AF255190

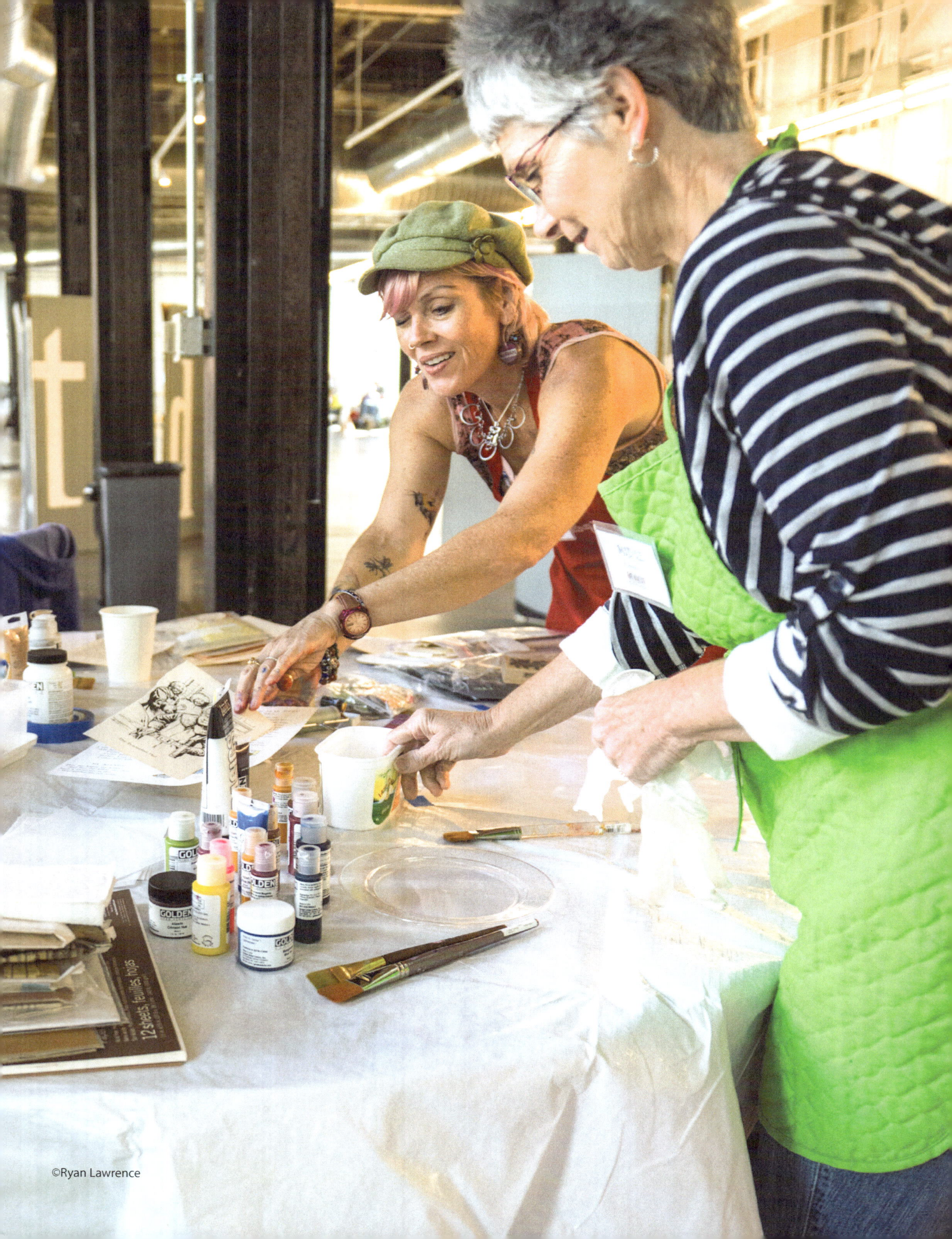
©Ryan Lawrence

Painterly
Gel Prints
Mono-printing plate how-to

ELIZABETH ST. HILAIRE

Making fine art prints with your Gel Press printing plate

Perfect for scrap booking, gift wrap, note cards, book covers, mobiles, and more!

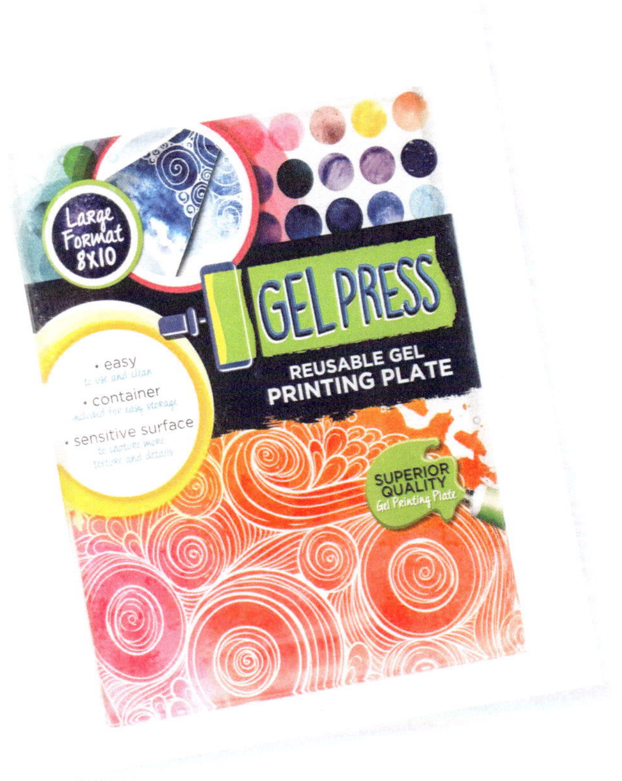

For Emilie and Connor

Thank you for loving me for who I am, for supporting me in what I do, and for understanding both.

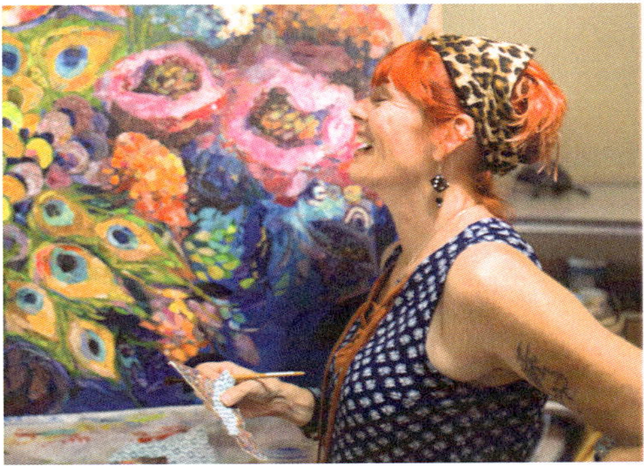

©Terri Zolinger

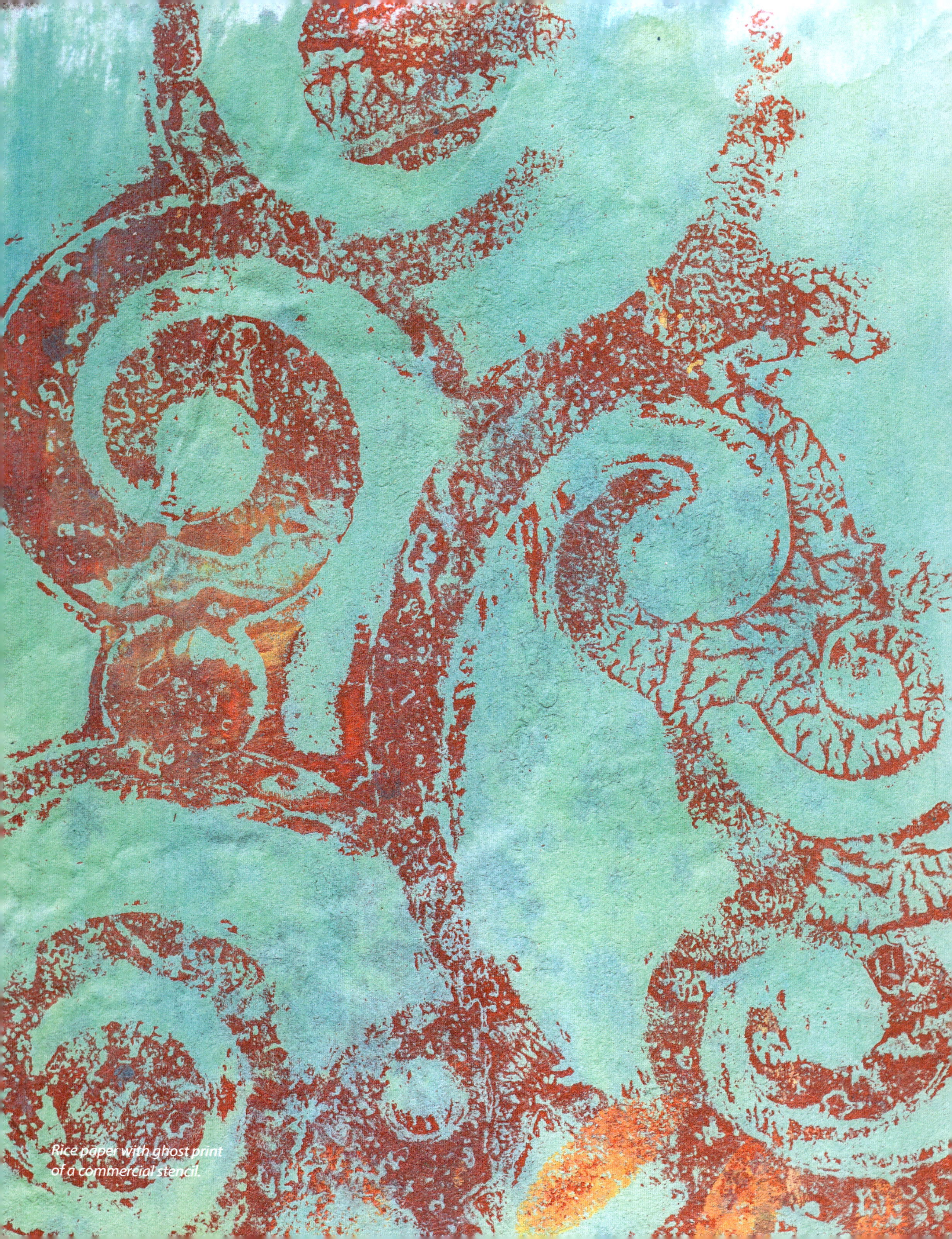

Rice paper with ghost print of a commercial stencil.

intro
getting started

The Gel Press printing plate has become all the rage with mixed media artists, and yet I find at least two or three people in my Paper Paintings Collage Workshop who have yet to experiment with it. You are in for a treat.

This Gel Press printing plate looks and feels like gelatin, but is durable, reusable and stores at room temperature. It doesn't take up room in your fridge and it's easy to clean and always ready for printing. Monoprinting on a Gel Press printing plate is simple and fun. The gratification is immediate, and the prints have endless creative uses.

It is my hope that you will experiment with all of the techniques in this book before you pick your favorites. The effects I get with some of my classroom demonstration papers make the students *ooh* and *ahhh*, but they don't necessarily always find them to be the techniques they choose to use themselves. Why not invite some friends to join you? Spread out a big table and have fun Gel printing papers together, then swap and trade and expand your inventory with the styles and color palettes of fellow paper decorators. I've gotten some of the best papers in trade that I would have never made on my own.

Enjoy the Journey,

Elizabeth St. Hilaire

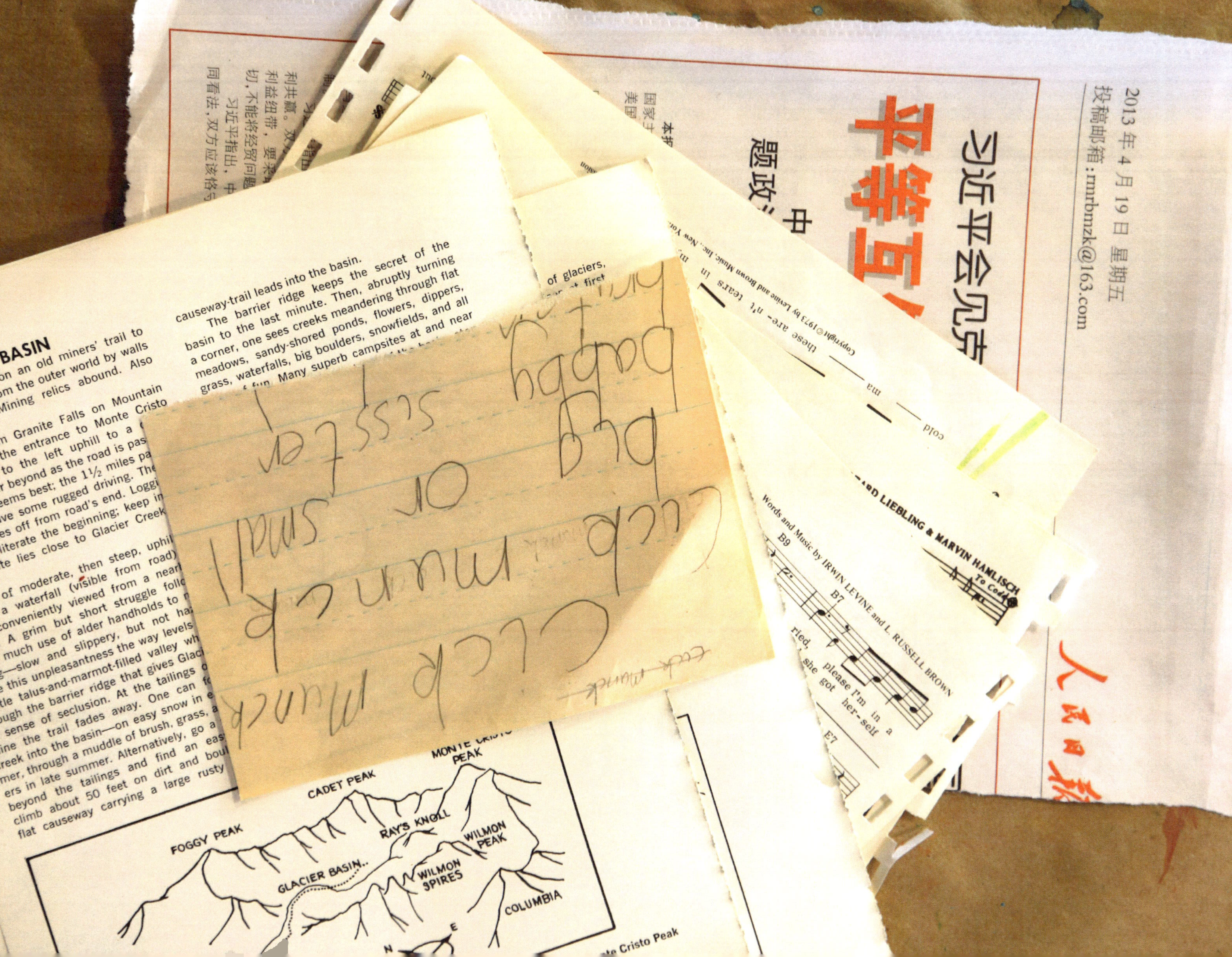
BASIN
on an old miners' trail to
from the outer world by walls
Mining relics abound. Also

om Granite Falls on Mountain
the entrance to Monte Cristo
to the left uphill to a
ar beyond as the road is pas
seems best; the 1½ miles pa
ave some rugged driving. The
kes off from road's end. Logg
bliterate the beginning; keep in
ute lies close to Glacier Creek

k of moderate, then steep, uphill
a waterfall (visible from a near
conveniently viewed from a near
p. A grim but short struggle follo
g much use of alder handholds to n
ng—slow and slippery, but not ha
ve this unpleasantness the way levels wh
ttle talus-and-marmot-filled valley wh
rough the barrier ridge that gives Glaci
s sense of seclusion. At the tailings o
nine the trail fades away. One can
creek into the basin—on easy snow in e
mer, through a muddle of brush, grass, a
ers in late summer. Alternatively, go a
beyond the tailings and find an eas
climb about 50 feet on dirt and boul
flat causeway carrying a large rusty

causeway-trail leads into the basin.
The barrier ridge keeps the secret of the
basin to the last minute. Then, abruptly turning
a corner, one sees creeks meandering through flat
meadows, sandy-shored ponds, flowers, dippers,
grass, waterfalls, big boulders, snowfields, and all
fun. Many superb campsites at and near
of glaciers,
first
FOGGY PEAK
CADET PEAK
MONTE CRISTO PEAK
RAY'S KNOLL
WILMON PEAK
GLACIER BASIN
WILMON SPIRES
COLUMBIA
N   E
Monte Cristo Peak
Cick Munck
Cick munck
big
babby
or small
sisster
LIEBLING & MARVIN HAMLISCH   To Coda
Words and Music by IRWIN LEVINE and L. RUSSELL BROWN
B9   B7   E7
please I'm in a
ried, she got her- self
these are   n't (tears) in   by Levine and Brown Music, Inc.   New Yo
Copyright 1973
cold   ma
2013 年 4 月 19 日 星期五
投稿邮箱:rmrbmzk@163.com
习近平会见克
平等互
中
题政
本报
国家主
美国
利共赢。双
利益纽带，要采
切,不能将经贸问题
习近平指出,中
同看法,双方应该恪
人民日报

paper
old and new

There are so many papers that are great for Gel printing!
Anything from standard copy bond to card stock to
printmaking paper to rice paper to old book pages.
I recommend starting out with inexpensive paper, as you
get used to Gel printing. You're going to go through a lot
of paper!

Bristol works well and makes an economical heavy paper.
Rives BFK or Rising Stonehenge are excellent printmaking
papers for fine prints and note cards. Deli paper (dry
waxed paper, available on *Amazon.com*) works much like
tissue paper due to its' thin, translucent properties.

I am also a fan of found papers, so check out your local
used book store or library for some old books that you can
take the pages out of. This paper is often great quality, the
text adds another layer to the creativity of the print making
process, and the books are inexpensive.

I have learned that glossy coated paper stock is not
compatible with the Gel Press printing plate. This type of
paper tends to stick to the plate and not come off without
damaging the plate's surface. DO NOT use any glossy
papers (including glossy photo papers).

Paper is such an individual preference, and your end
purpose will be a factor in your paper choice. A smooth-
surfaced paper gives a more detailed print.

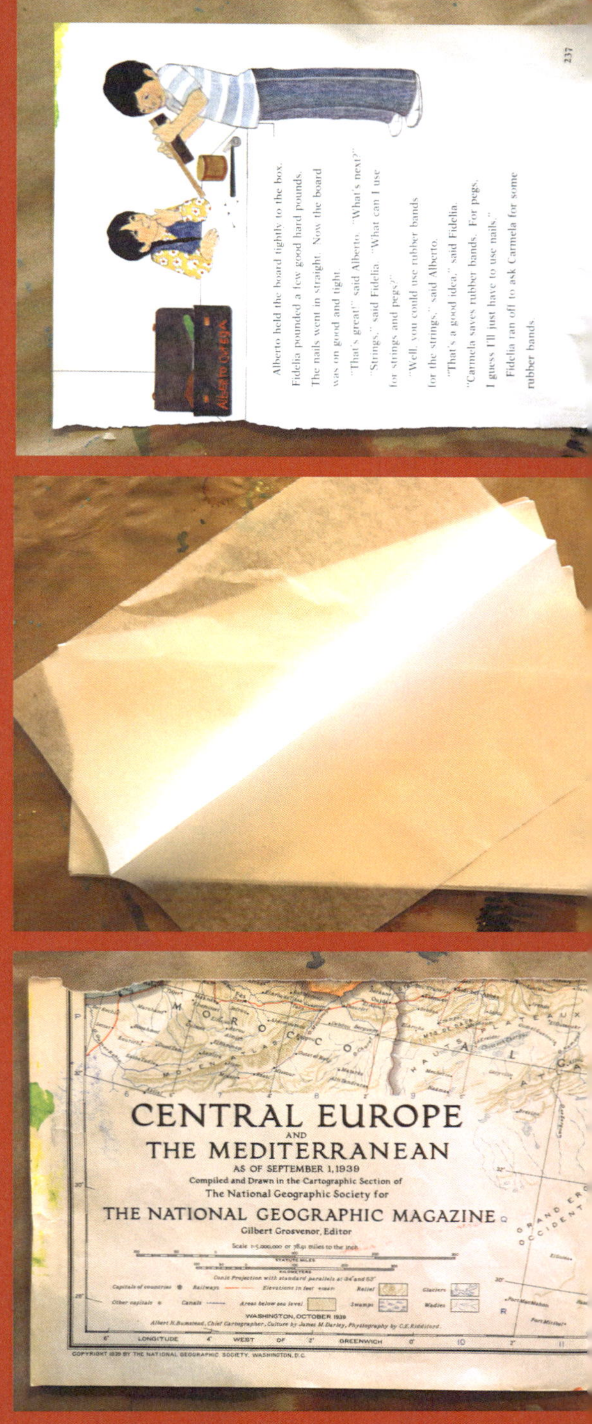

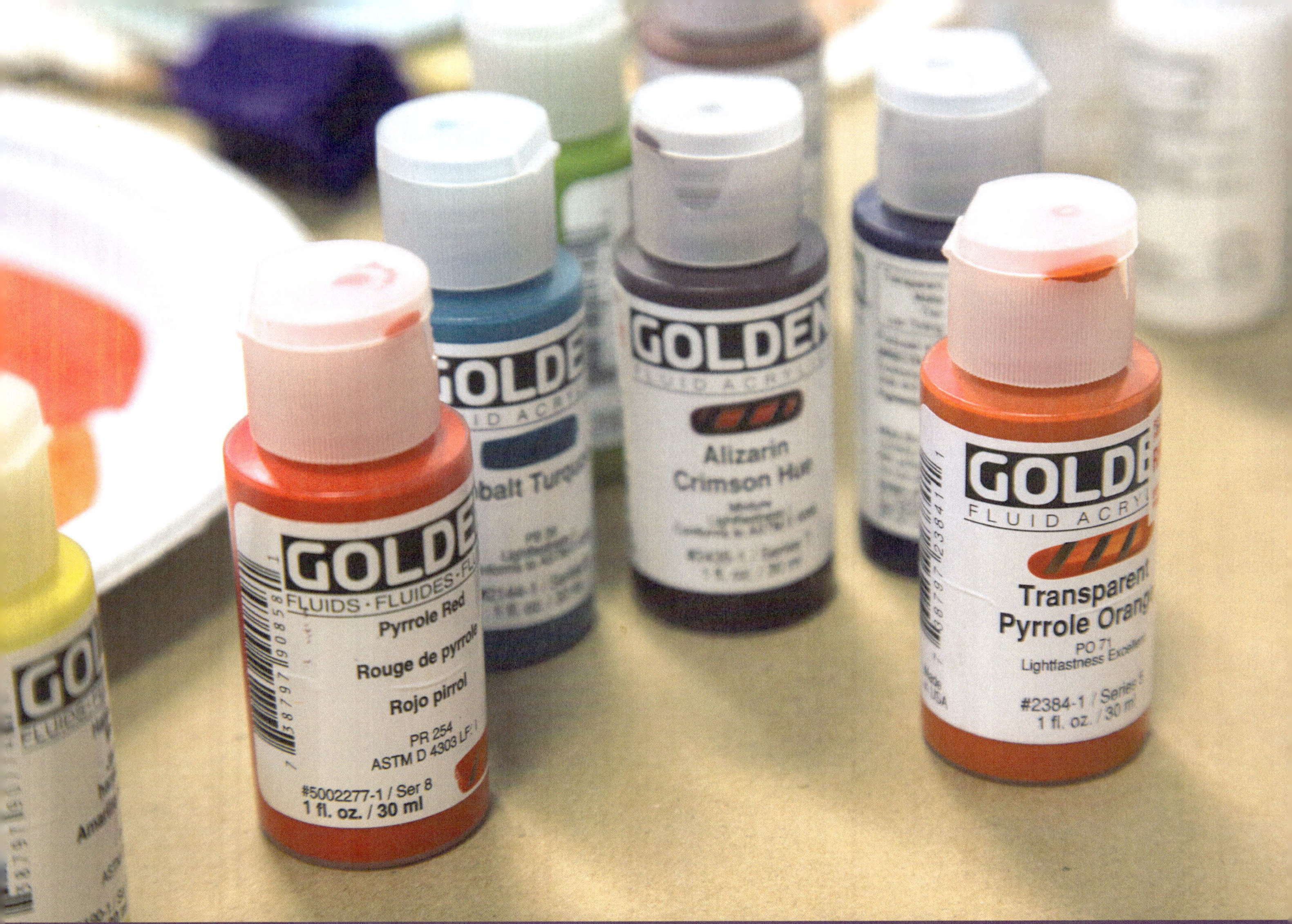

paint

As I have mentioned, I prefer to use Golden Fluid Acrylic colors to paint my papers. These paints are light fast, durable, and flexible. They are wonderfully versatile, professional quality acrylic colors with the consistency of heavy cream. Visit them on-line and request a color swatch chart for accurate color representation: *GoldenPaints.com*

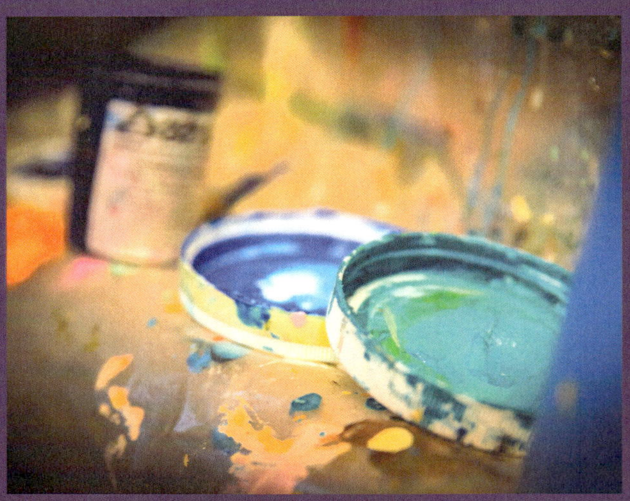

Fluid Acrylics are translucent, this is important. In this book, every layer of the mono printing process allows the previous layer to shine through. This is the effect of translucent paints, they multiply and blend in the print.

Another brand I like is Nova Color out of Culver City, CA. I have visited the factory store and the paints are very high quality. Nova Color caters to mural painters, so you can get your favorite color from a small container all the way up to a gallon if you like. Visit them on-line and request a color swatch chart for accurate color representation: *NovaColorPaint.com*

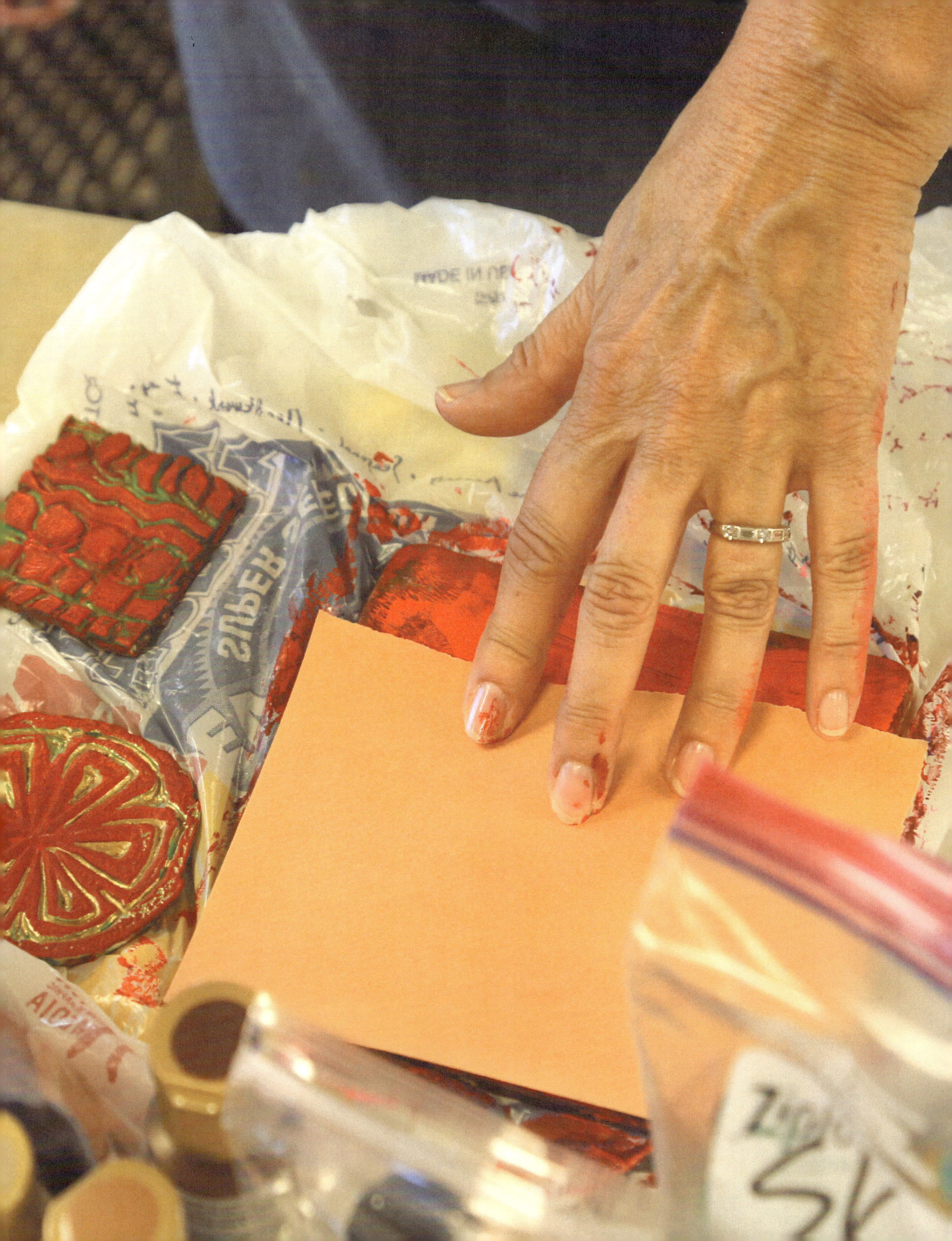

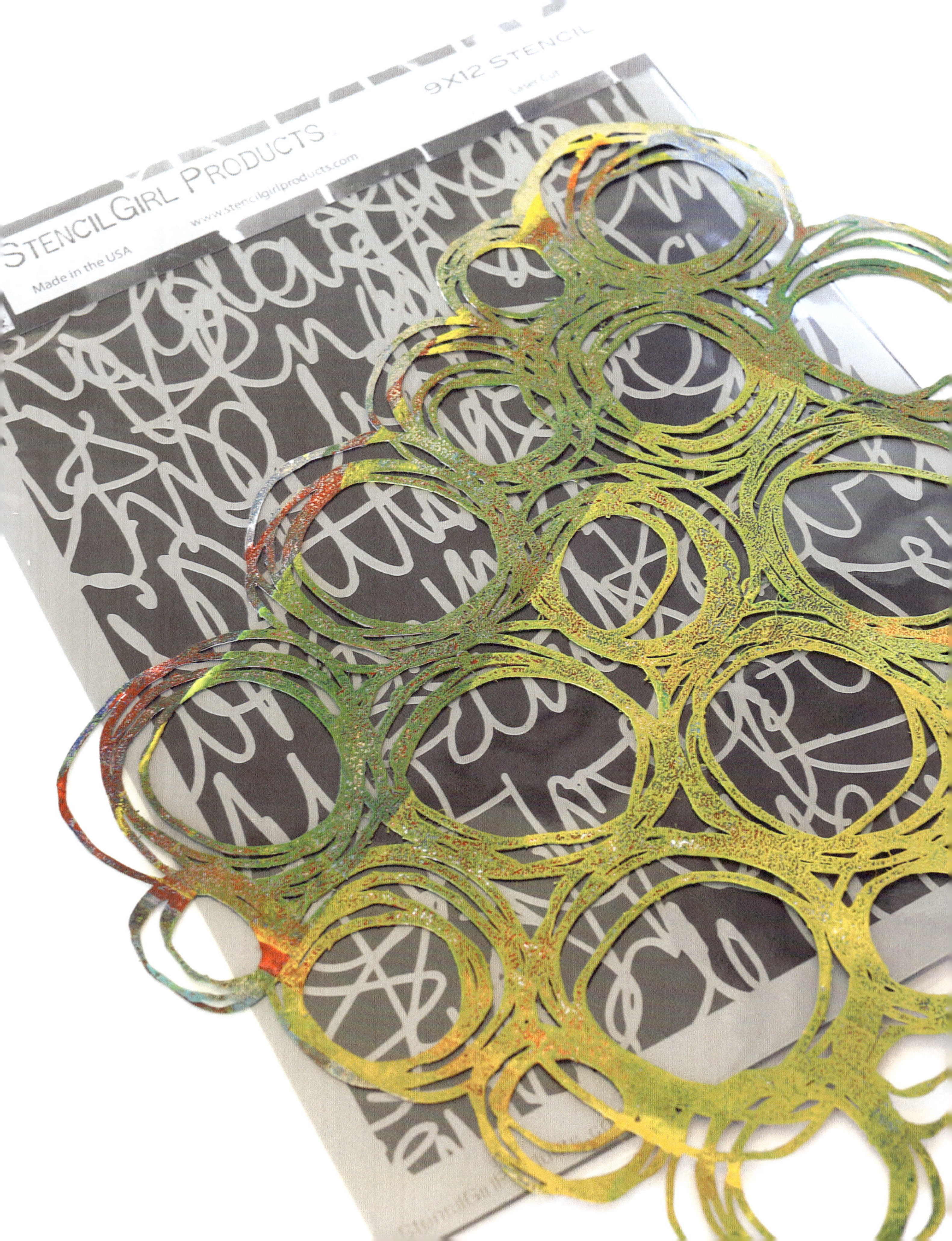

StencilGirl PRODUCTS
www.stencilgirlproducts.com
Made in the USA
9X12 STENCIL

experi-menting

nothing is off limits!

They key to learning new techniques with the Gel Press printing plate is experimentation. Most of the techniques presented in this book are a result of many hours of playing with the plate, the paints, and the tools. Some concepts have worked out better than others, and some have been total flops! But that does not discourage me from trying new things every time I pull out the Gel Press printing plate and the box of tools in my studio.

Often times, it's a happy accident that leads the way to a new technique, this is why experimenting is so important. Although, sometimes it's very difficult to reproduce that happy accident with quite the same results!

I love the effect of commercial stencils on the plate, but off-the-wall materials can also make for interesting and unique results. The more you lean toward utilizing unique materials, the more different your prints look from other artists' work.

My favorite commercial stencil resource is: _StencilGirlProducts.com_ where Mary Beth and her husband work directly with artists to design their products, and sell them only in small shops or on-line.

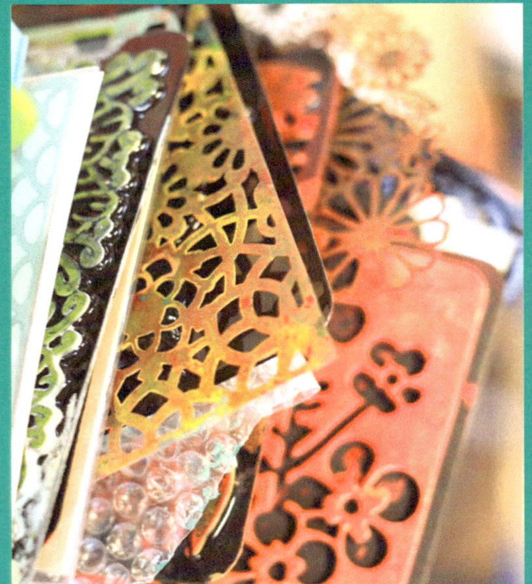
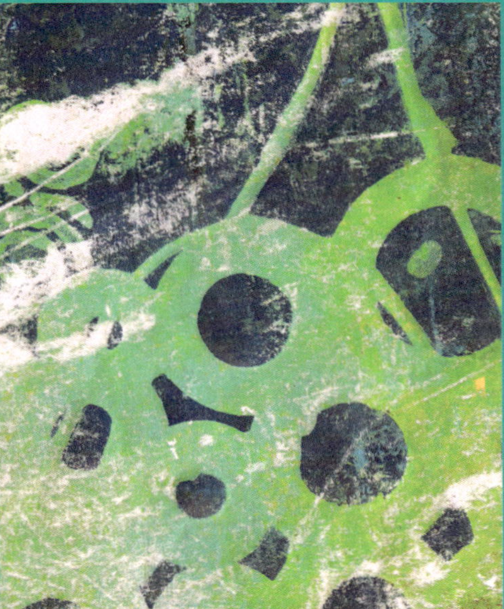
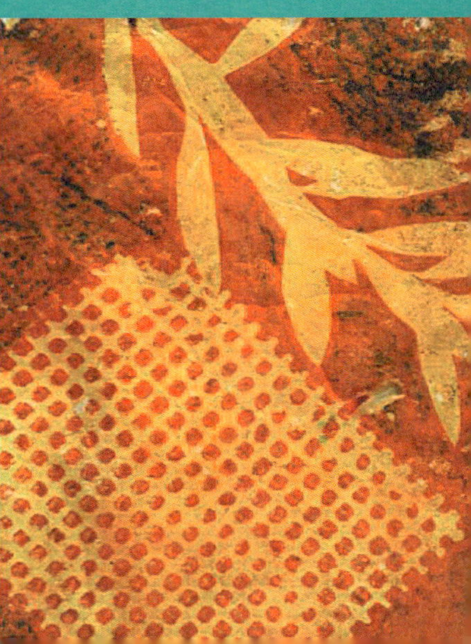

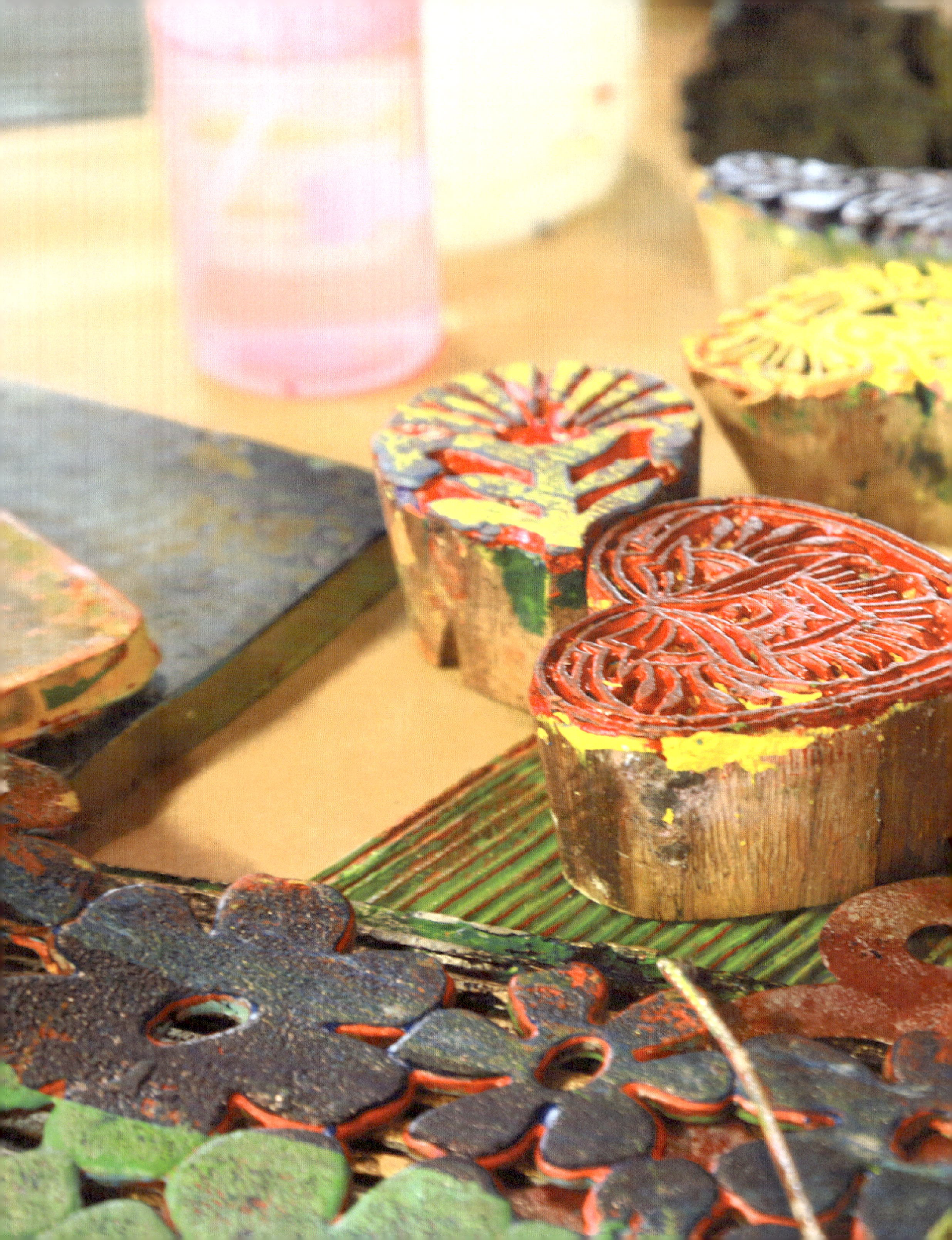

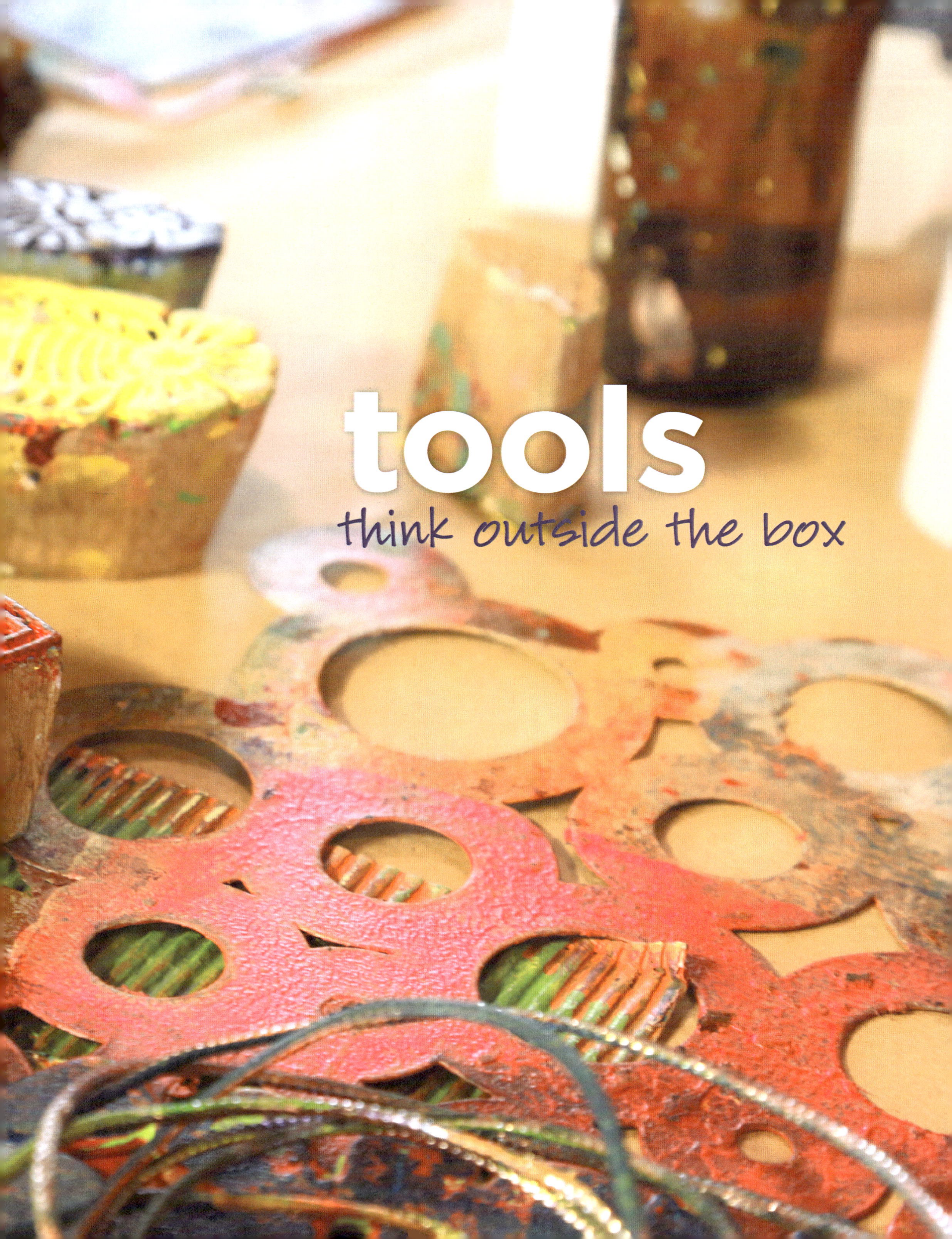
tools
think outside the box

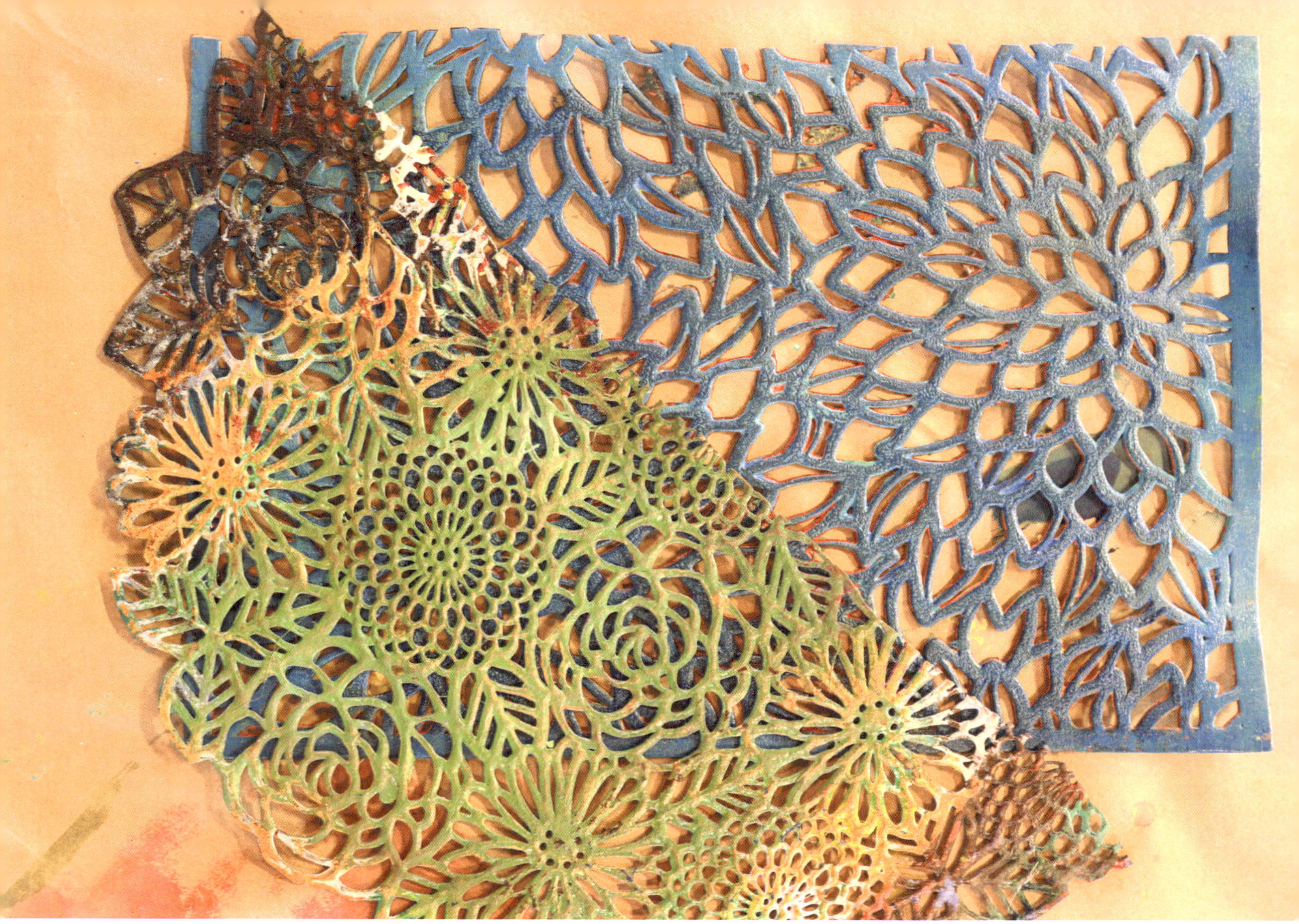

kitchen items

Often times household and home improvement store items make excellent art supplies. Above are two place-mats (each cut in half) made from a flexible silicone material which works wonderful with the Gel Press printing plate. These were at my local Old Time Pottery store, which is very similar to a Tuesday Morning on steroids.

On the right is a silicone sink liner, purchased at Lowe's Home Improvement. One day I was wandering around Lowe's and came across this beauty on an end cap. I noticed the pattern first, then the material. Upon experimenting with this liner on my Gel Press printing plate, I enjoyed the results so much that went on-line and ordered several more in varying patterns and sizes.

Every now and then I am lucky enough to pick up sink liners and place-mats up at my local Marshall's store at a discount.

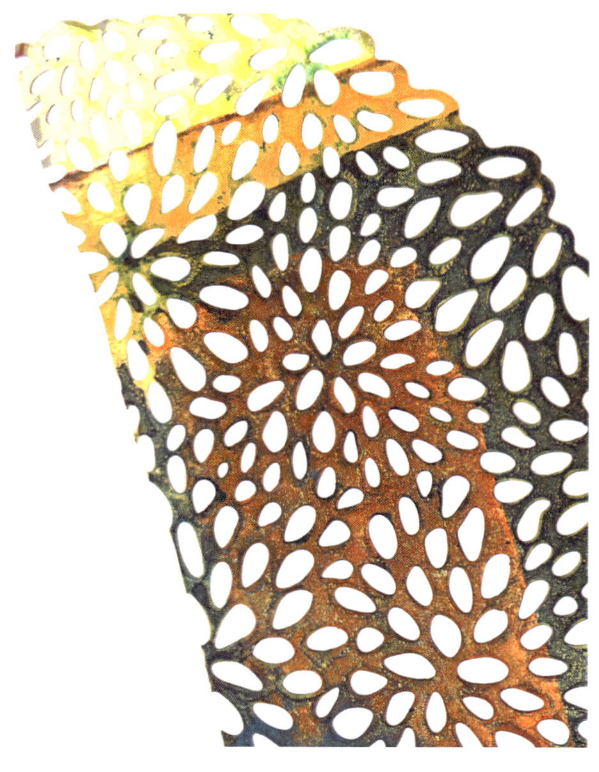

stencils

Whether you choose to purchase commercial stencils, or try your hand at making one of your own, they offer hours of experimenting fun with your Gel Press printing plate.

The commercial stencils shown below are well loved and coated with paint from my many workshop students. These stencils were purchased exclusively from *StencilGirlProducts.com* and have traveled around the world with me as part of my workshop supply box. I love the durability and extra fine details that Stencil Girl stencils have to offer.

When working in the studio, it's a good idea to have a dish basin full of soapy warm water to toss your stencils (and other tools) in between usage. Keeping your stencils clean will help to preserve their longevity by keeping the very small detailed areas from filling in with acrylic paint--this can eventually ruin the stencil. Rubbing alcohol can be very effective in loosening dried acrylic paint so that you have success in scrubbing it off.

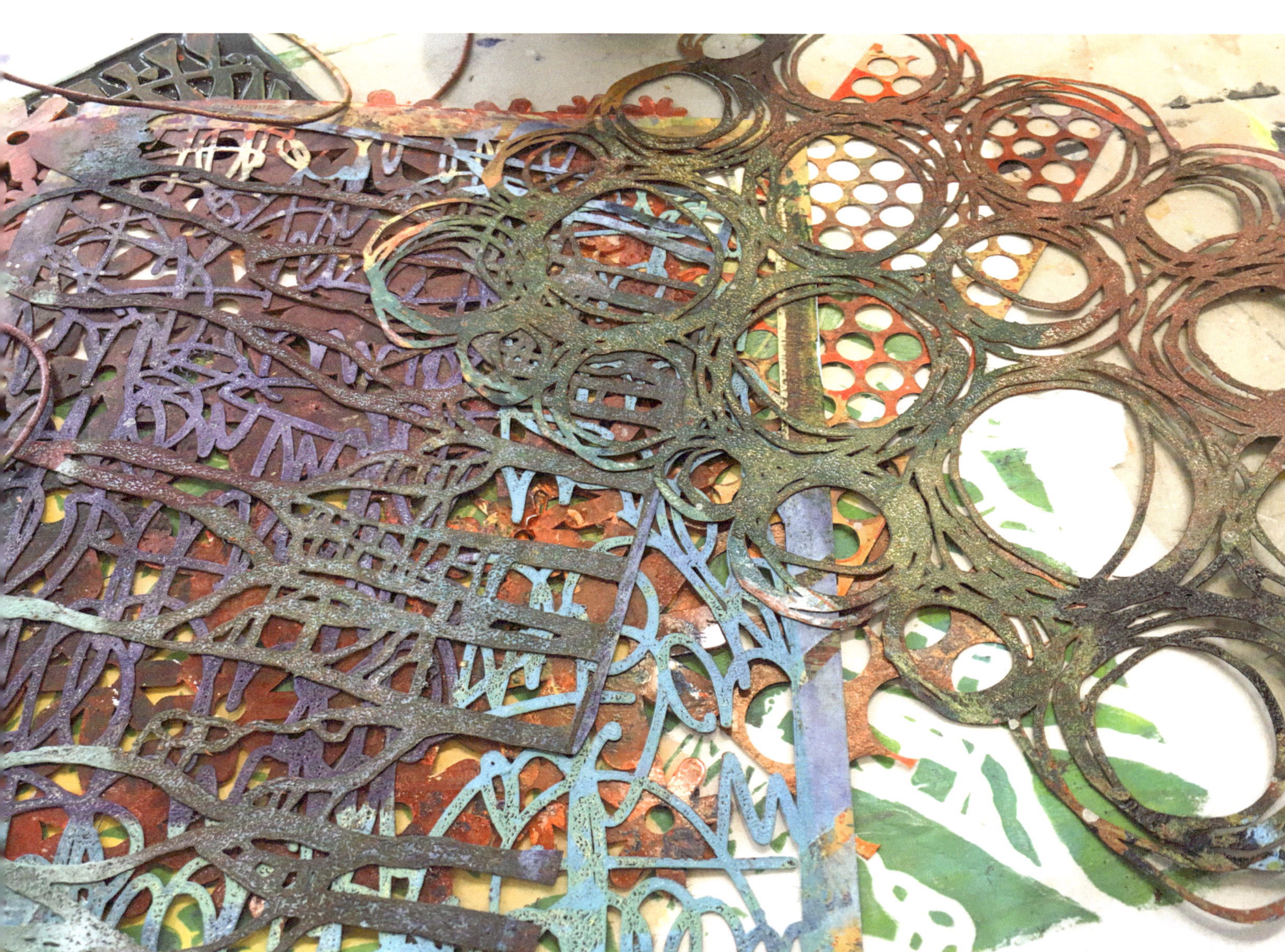

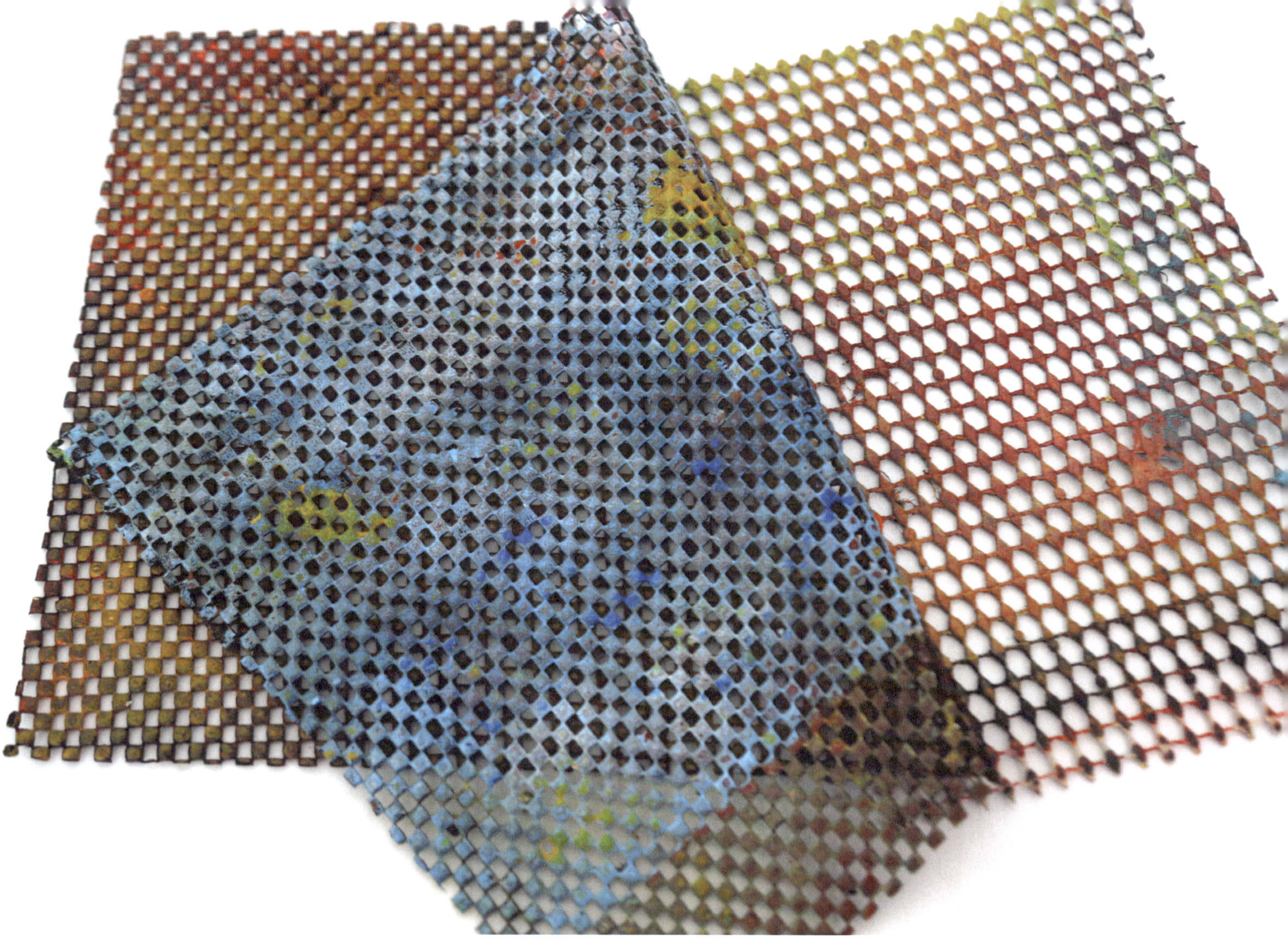

non slip liners

Shelf and carpet liners are made of a wonderful squishy material that works well with the Gel Press printing plate both as a mask and to pick up color. The carpet liner, with it's larger pattern, makes a wonderful masking tool, whereas the shelf liner offers a small dot pattern and works better in removing paint in a pattern.

I typically purchase both on a roll at my local Target store, using a small piece until it's covered with paint and worn out. A roll of this material will go a long way and offer endless experimentation with your Gel Press printing plate.

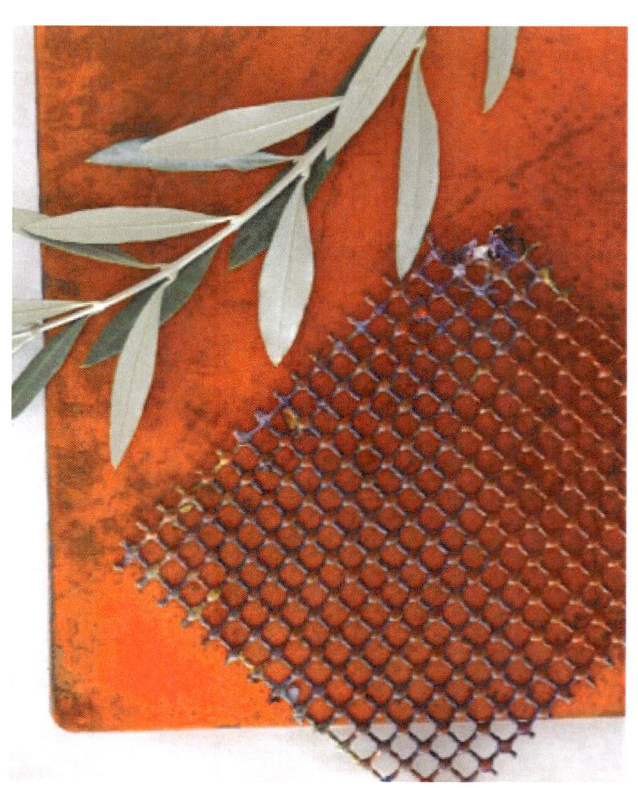

carved stamps

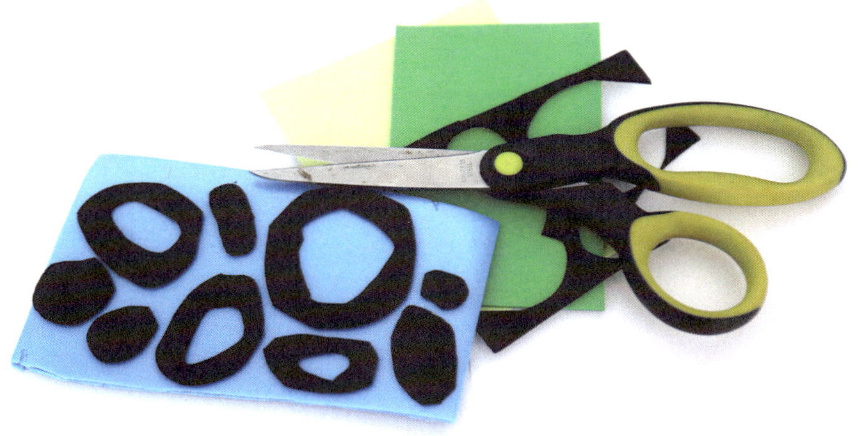

The stamps above are cut from self adhesive fun foam, with scissors. This foam is easy to cut and typically available in the kids craft section of your local Jo-Ann or Michael's craft store. Simply cut the foam into shapes that are appealing to you, peel off the backing, and stick them to cardboard, chipboard, or a second piece of foam. I have even adhered this foam to a rolling pin or a cardboard paper towel tube for continuous rolling patterns.

Below are stamps carved from various soft carving pad material such as *Speedball Carving Pad* or *Blick Redicut*. This soft, flexible carving material is easily cut with traditional linoleum carving tools, both are typically available in the block printing section of your local art supply store.

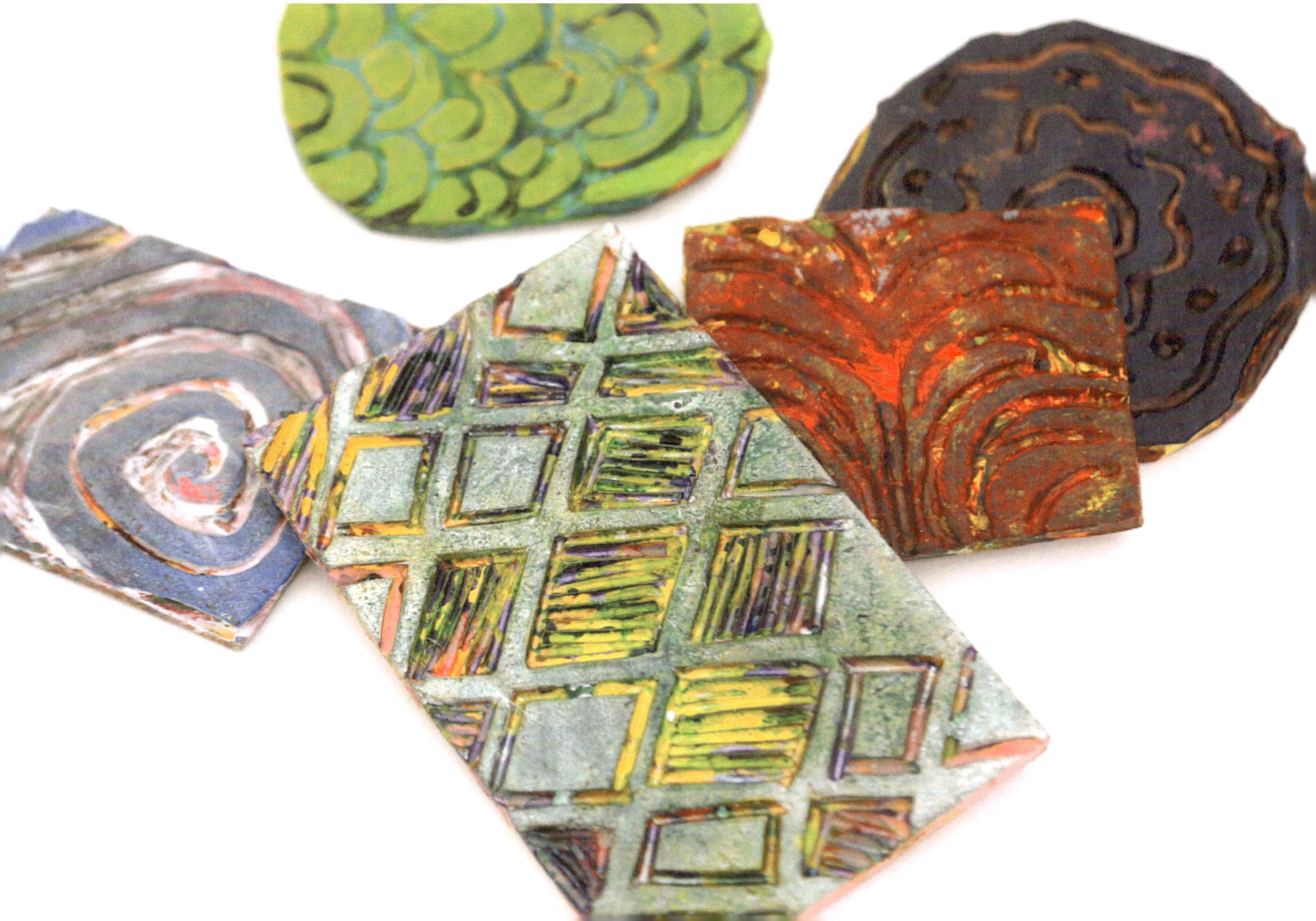

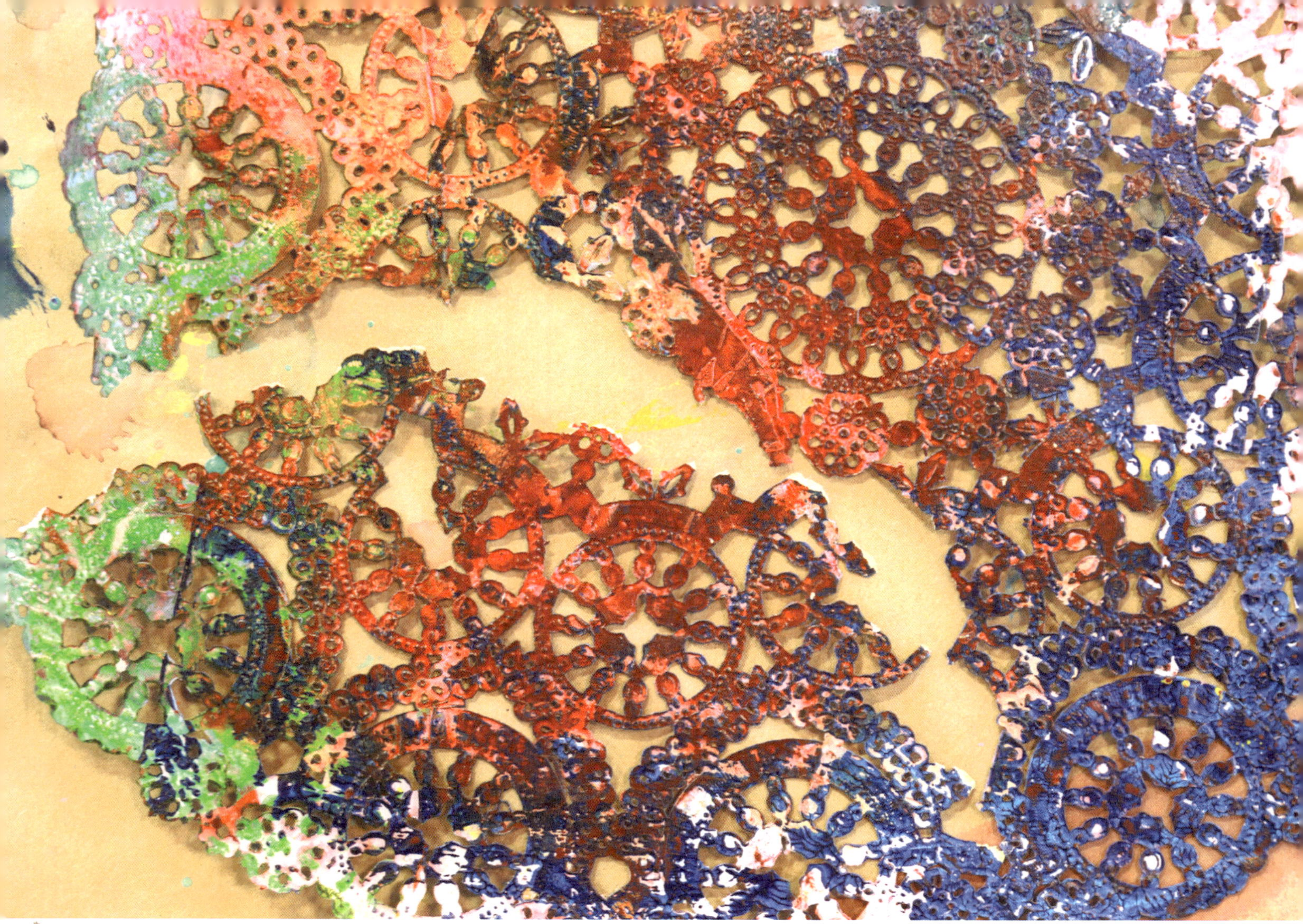

paper products

Above is a well loved, overused paper doily that has been in my workshop box for almost a year. Coating the doily on both sides with gesso primer before using it on your Gel Press printing plate will help it to last longer as it will be protected from moisture. The doily works well as a mask, offering varying patterns depending on what brand and size you purchase. Look for commercial doilies at restaurants or at restaurant supply, that are larger and are often times fully patterned (without a solid center circle), like the one shown above.

On the right is a piece of corrugated cardboard with the top layer of paper removed. Different boxes have different corrugation patterns, thick and thin.

As with the doily, I coat the corrugated cardboard sheet on both sides with gesso primer before using, to protect from moisture and to extend its life as an art supply material.

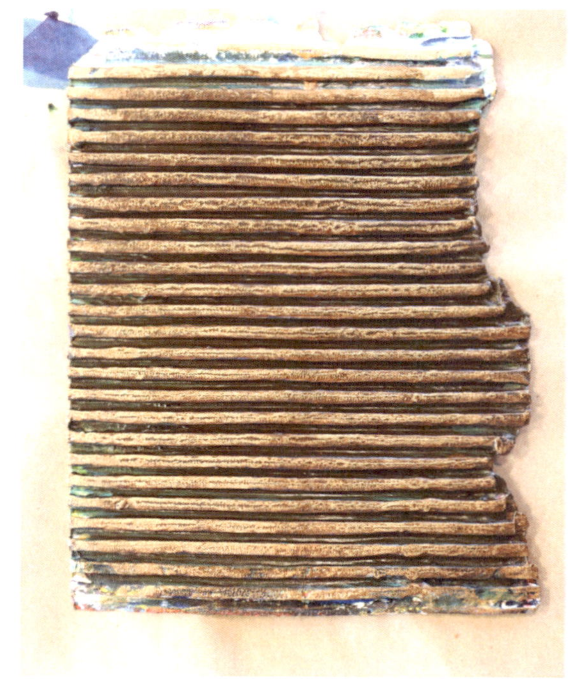

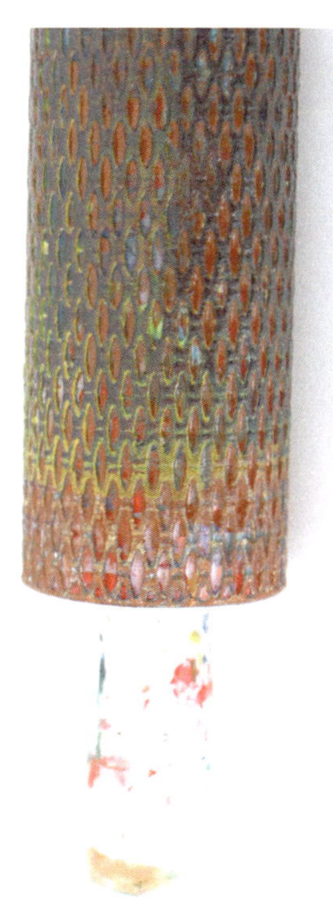

textured surfaces

To the left is an embossed rolling pin for cake decorating. Typically used for fondant fronsting; these rolling pins make a wonderul patterned texture on the Gel Press plate, and come in many patterns.

Below are two examples of plastic texture plates purchased on-line. These plates are useful for removing paint in a distinct, yet subtle pattern on the Gel Press printing plate. Available in many patterns, these plates offer endless texture possibilities for Gel printing.

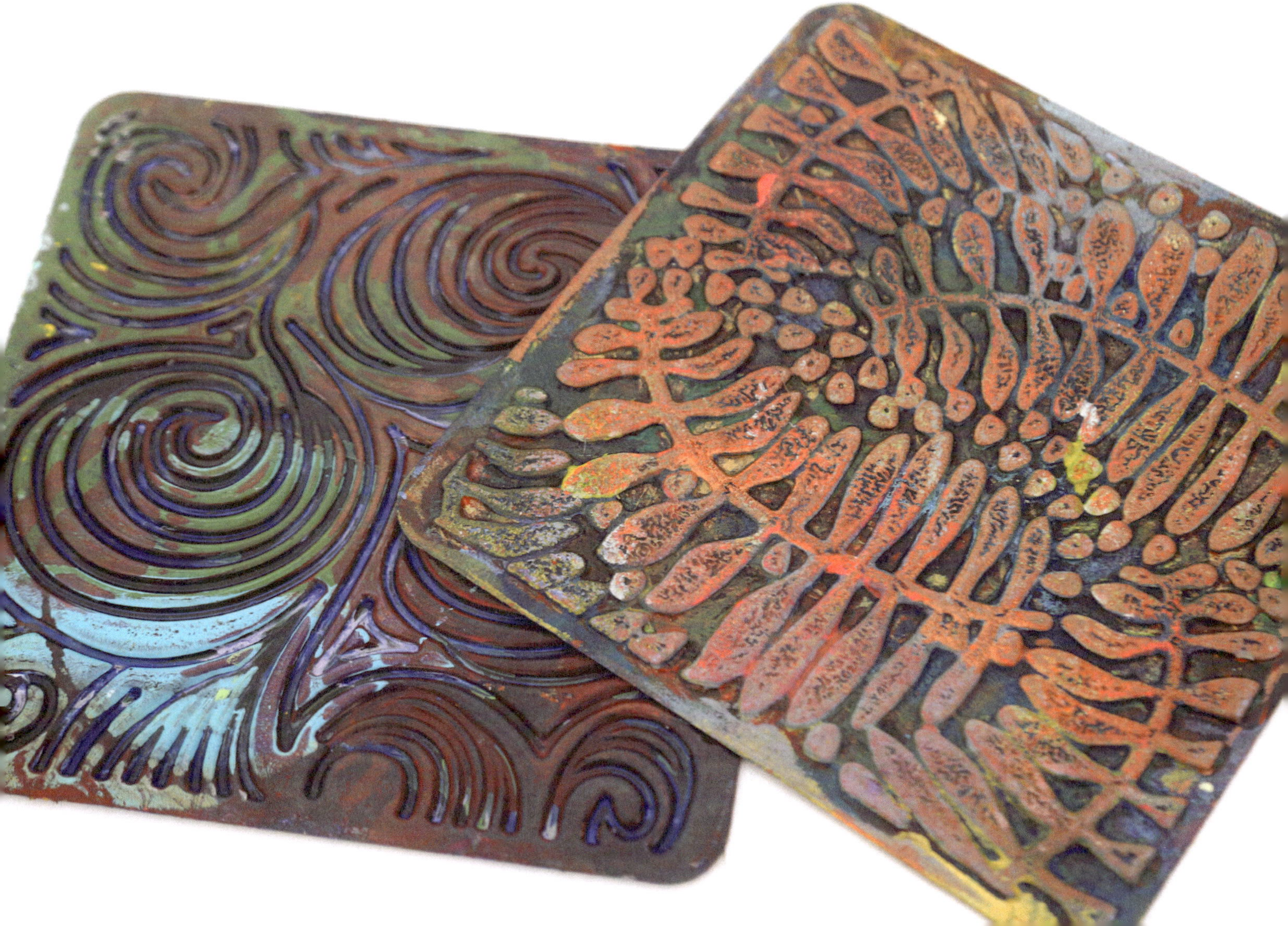

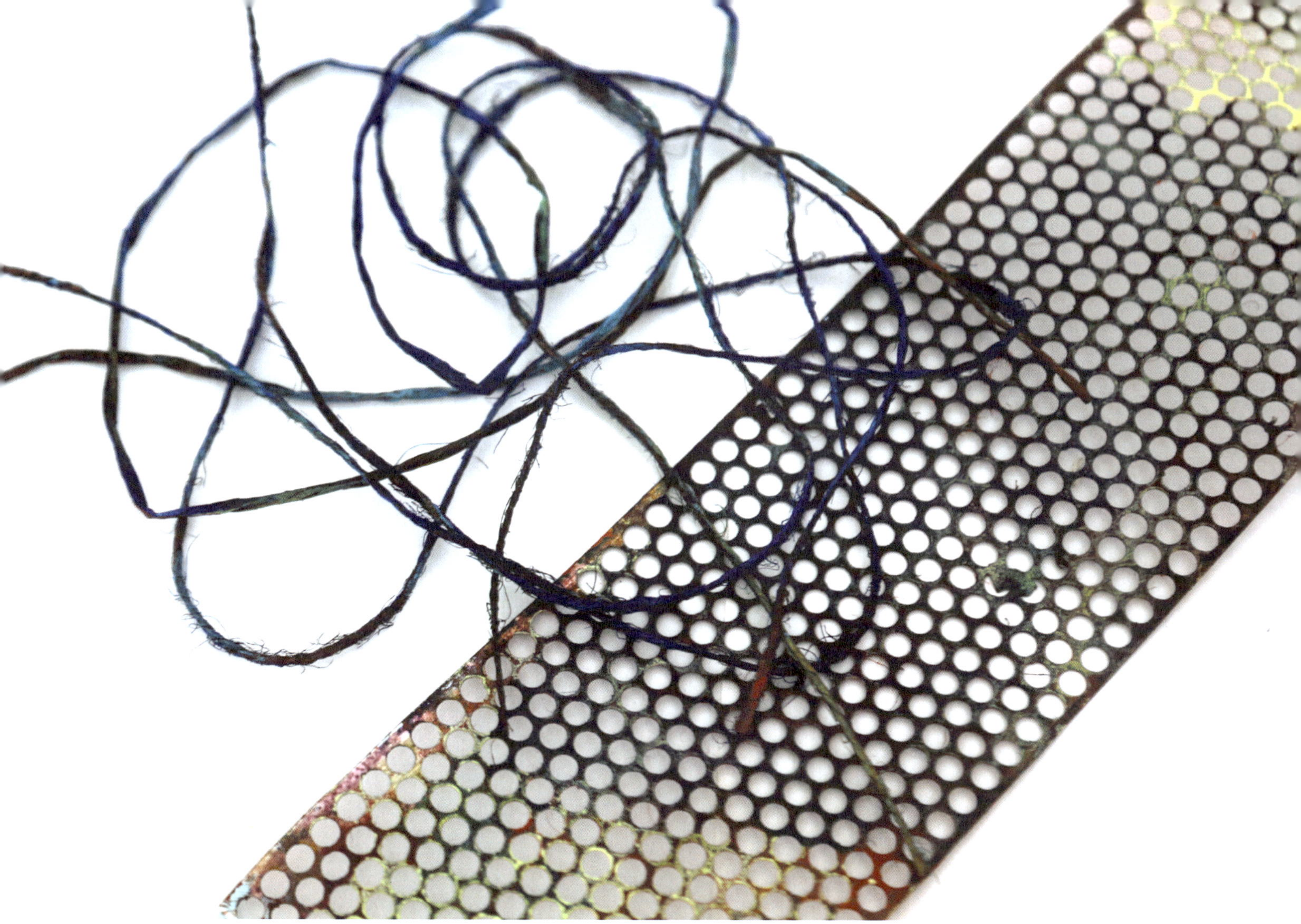

found objects

String works wonderfully as a mask on the Gel Press printing plate and can be contorted into endless patterns. The gift string above is metallic and cylindrical. Other strings that work well include yarn, shoe laces, kite string, zig zag fabric trim, etc.

The material with the hole pattern is called sequin waste, or *punchinella*. This is the material left behind from sequins being punched out. You can typically find this at your local craft store, I call it a *found object* here because there are similar materials around your home with such patterns, look at everything with a different perspective now that you have purchased your Gel Press printing plate.

The fibrous blue material to the right is similar to an onion bag (which also may be utilized), it was found at a fabric store by an interior designer friend who thought it might make a better art supply than fabric!

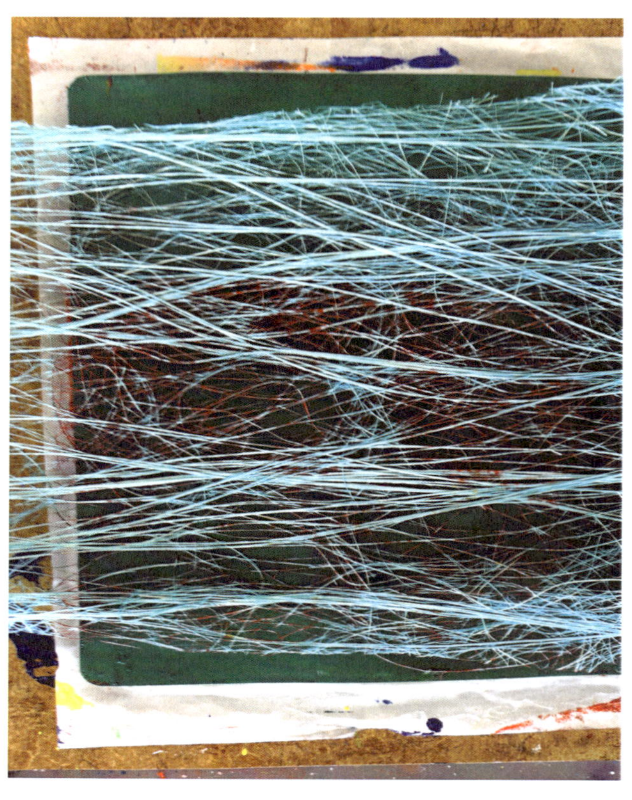

brayers

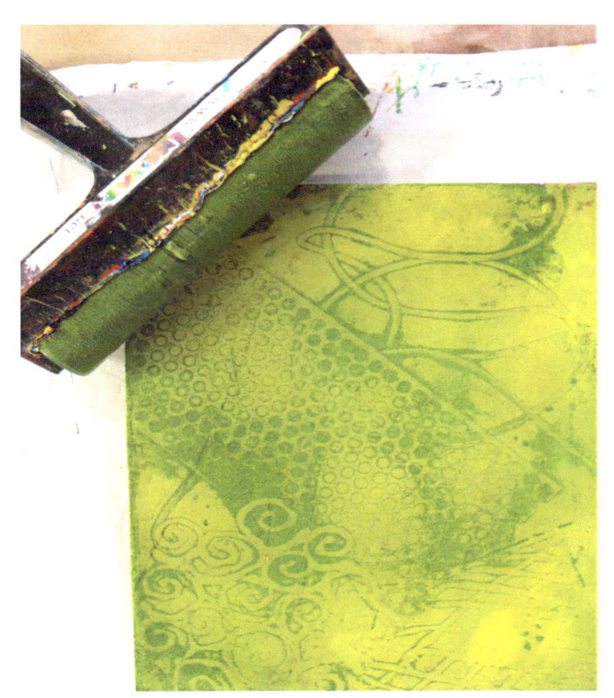

Brayers are used to apply a thin layer of paint to your Gel Press printing plate, thin is key. These well loved (and colorful) brayers were purchased at *DickBlick. com* and are basic soft foam rollers by Inovart. Foam rollers are inexpensive and work well in my traveling workshop supply box, however you may want to invest in a better quality piece of equipment for your studio. Speedball makes some nice heavy duty brayers.

The best way to keep a brayer clean between paint layers on your Gel Press printing plate is to roll it off onto a clean sheet of paper and onto a wet paper towel. That sheet of paper may eventually work as a base layer for some interesting mono-printing, so don't throw it away. I roll excess paint from my brayer onto the pages of an old book.

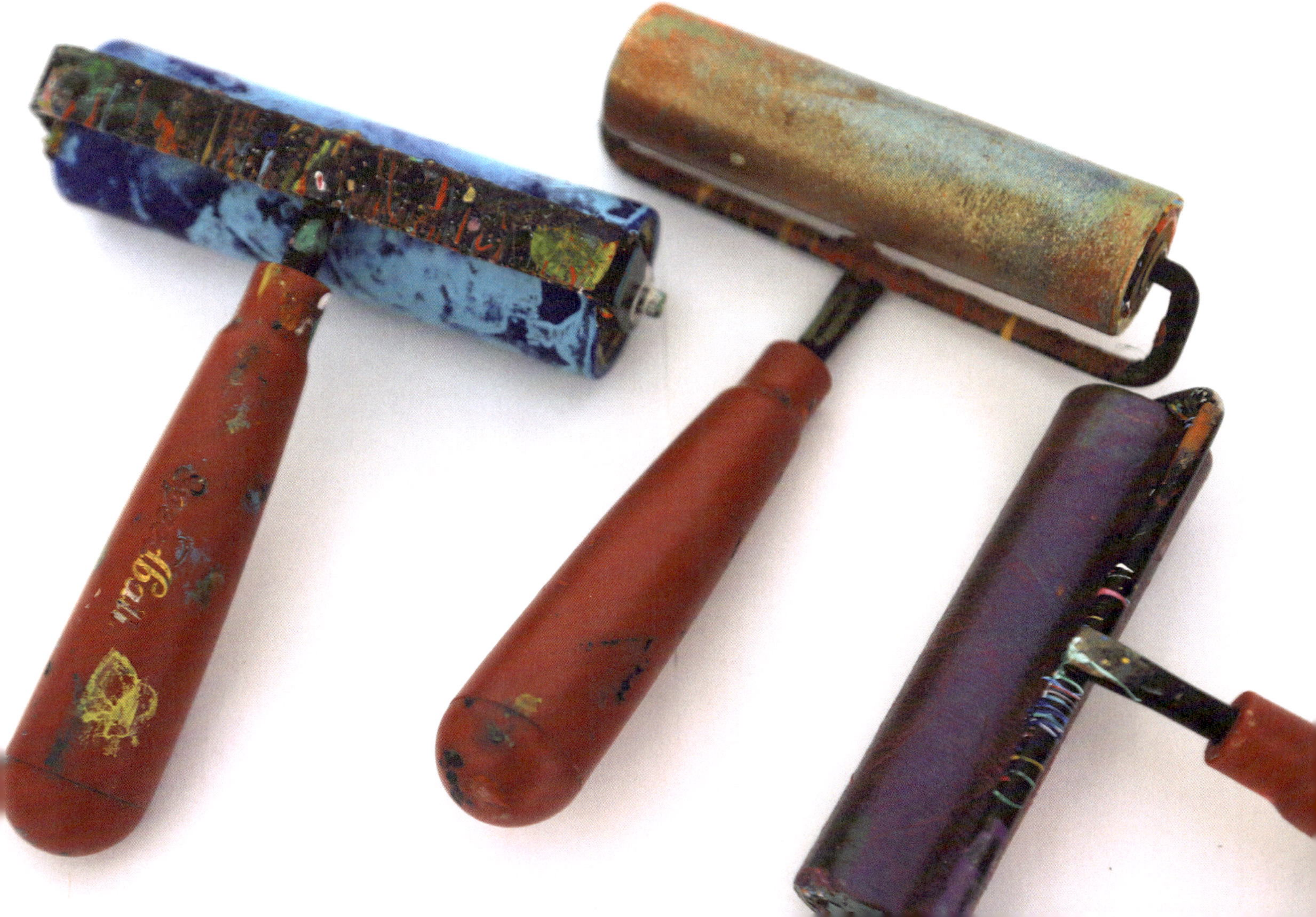

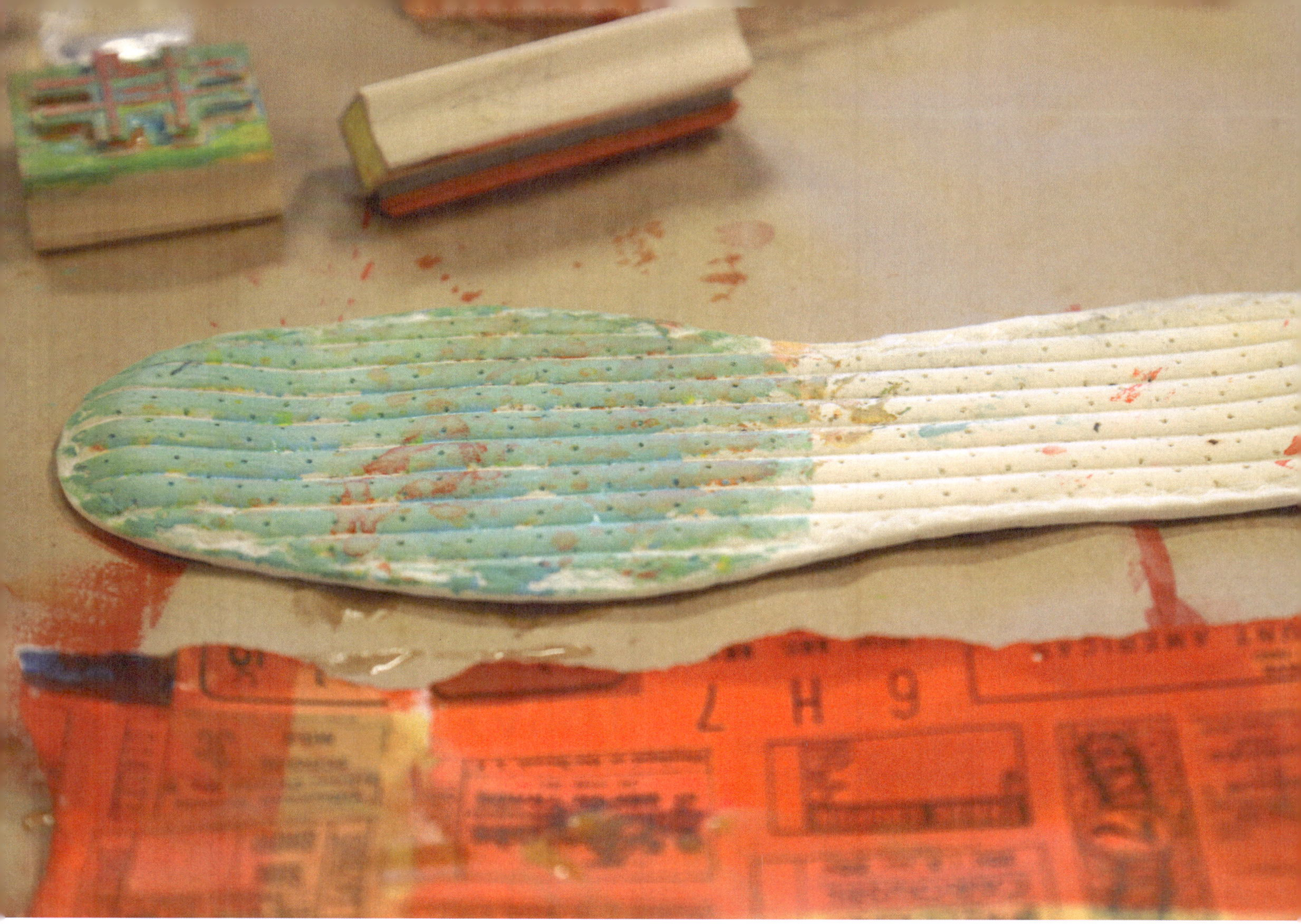

the unexpected

In my last workshop, Dottie brought along her son-in-law's shoe insoles to use as a texture plate. She had come in from out of town and was staying with her family in order to attend my class. Dottie was encouraged to look in unexpected places for art making materials because she wasn't able to travel with as much of her art supplies as she wanted to.

I've had resourceful students bring potato mashers, flip flop soles, glass tile samples, faux painting tools, toilet paper rolls, kitchen sponges, cross stitch material... Nothing is off limits, so think outside the art supply box!

On the right are two wooden snow flake ornaments that my students from Massachusetts traveled to Italy with. The ornaments were hand-made by their uncle and in the family for years. Thank you Joni and Maryann!

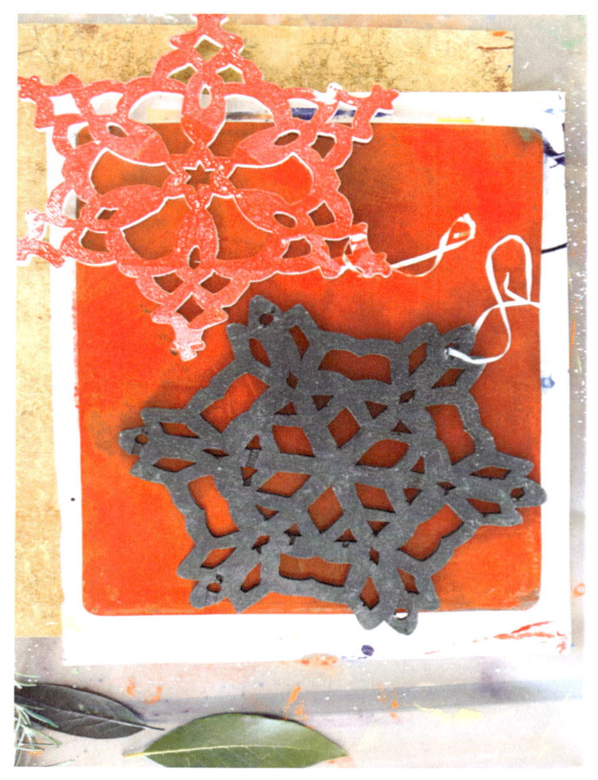

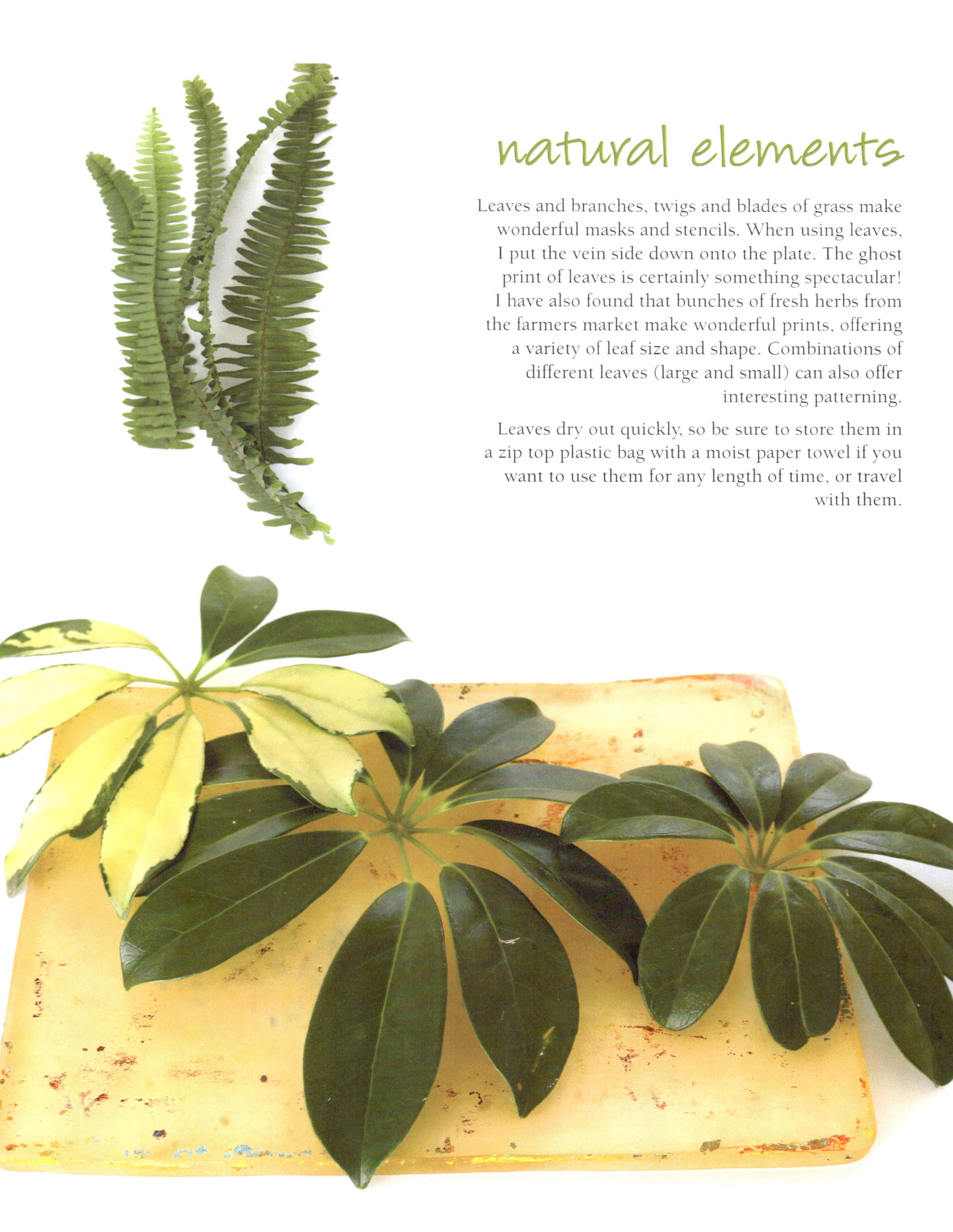

natural elements

Leaves and branches, twigs and blades of grass make wonderful masks and stencils. When using leaves, I put the vein side down onto the plate. The ghost print of leaves is certainly something spectacular! I have also found that bunches of fresh herbs from the farmers market make wonderful prints, offering a variety of leaf size and shape. Combinations of different leaves (large and small) can also offer interesting patterning.

Leaves dry out quickly, so be sure to store them in a zip top plastic bag with a moist paper towel if you want to use them for any length of time, or travel with them.

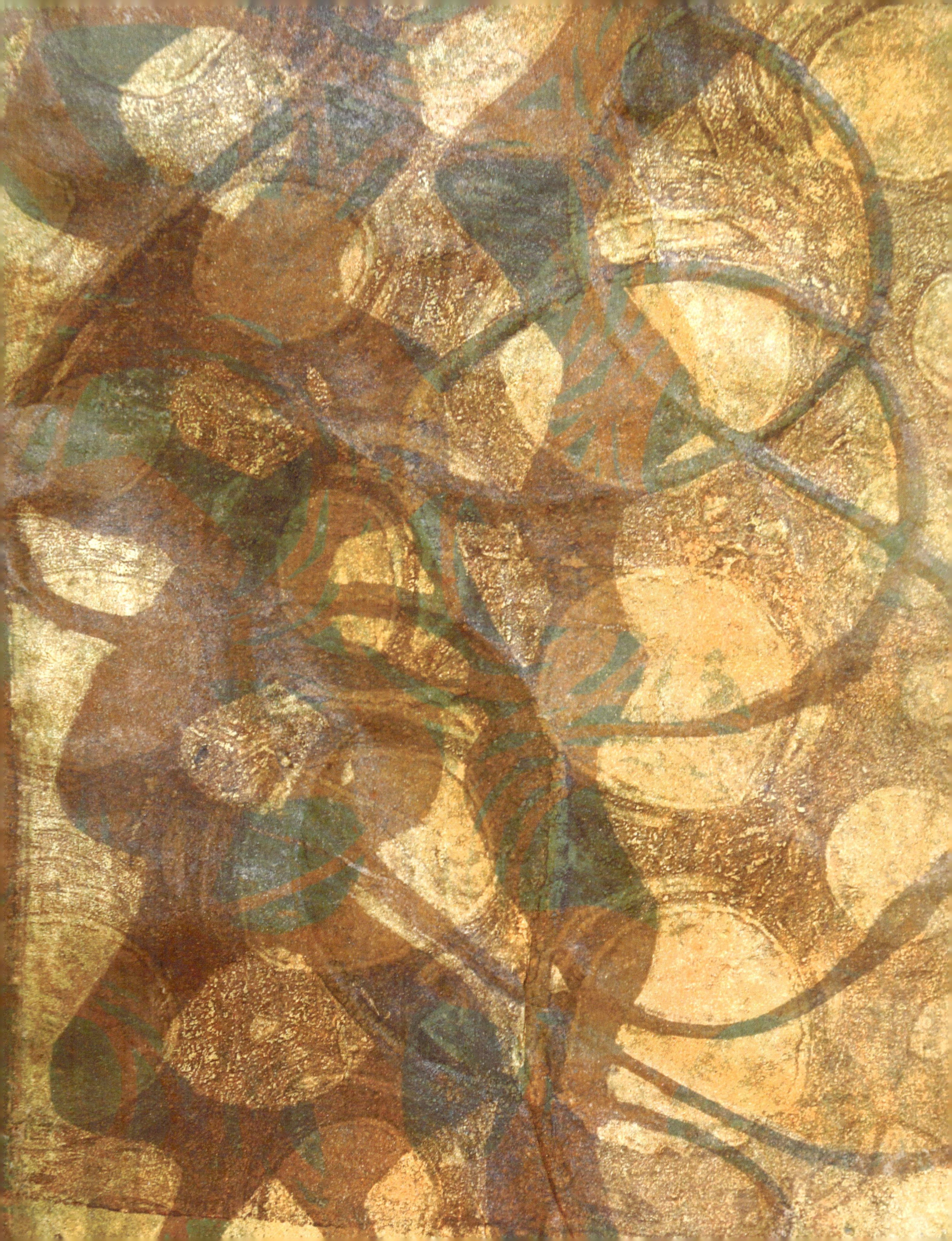

color
combinations

Starting with light colors and working your way down to darker colors is the way to go with fluid acrylics, which are the paints I prefer in my process. Because fluid acrylics are translucent, a light color will not show up very well over a darker color. For this reason, I start light and every subsequent layer is a little darker. I also like to use colors that are next to each other on the color wheel for harmony, or colors that are across from each other for discord. I suggest experimenting with both to see what appeals to you.

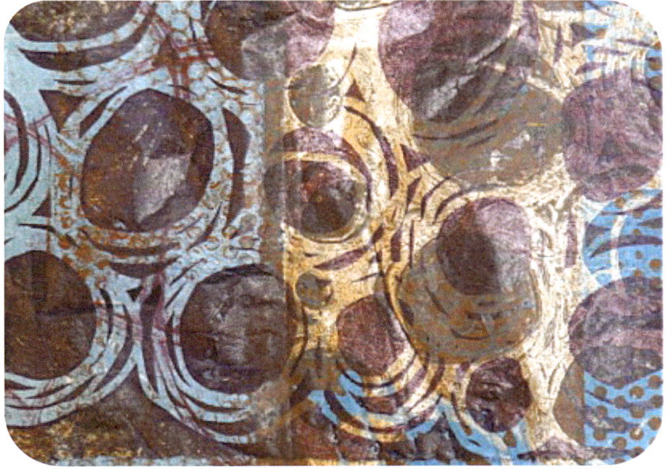

Harmonious colors start with light blue,
to dark purple, to opaque gold on top.

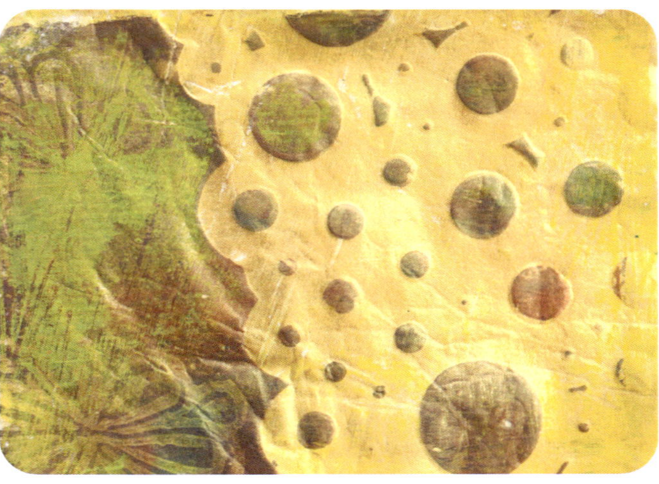

Creating an overall glow by utilizing metallic paint for
the base and translucent, darker colors on top.

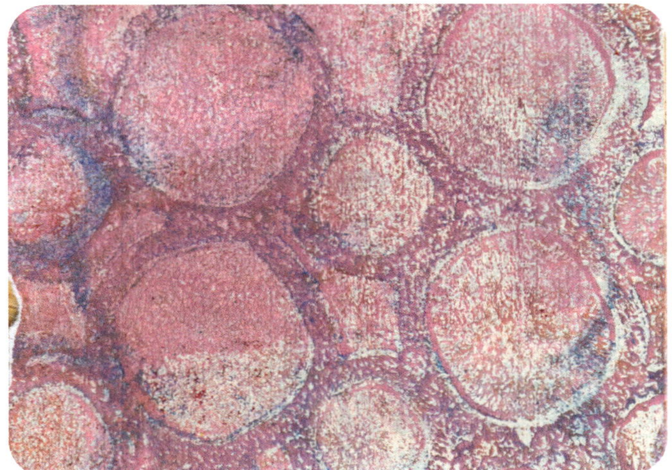

Creating harmony by staying with colors that are next
to each other on the color wheel. Staring with magenta
and adding darker purple layers.

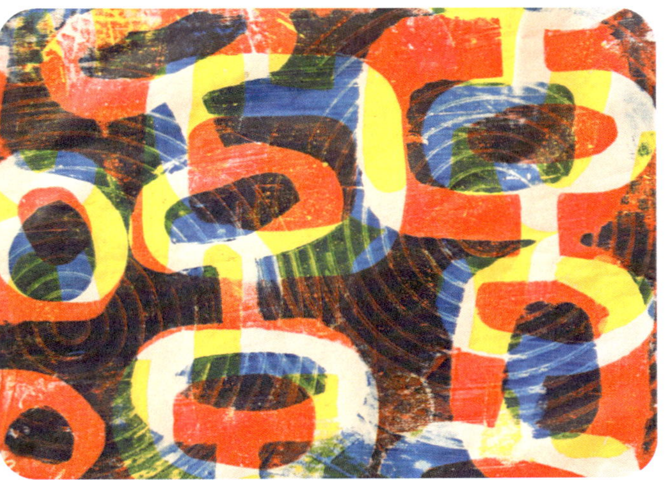

Creating discord with opposite colors.
Starting with yellow, adding red, and lastly blue.
Working light to dark, the base layer being white.

Some excellent color wheel information: www.tigercolor.com/color-lab/color-theory/color-theory-intro.htm

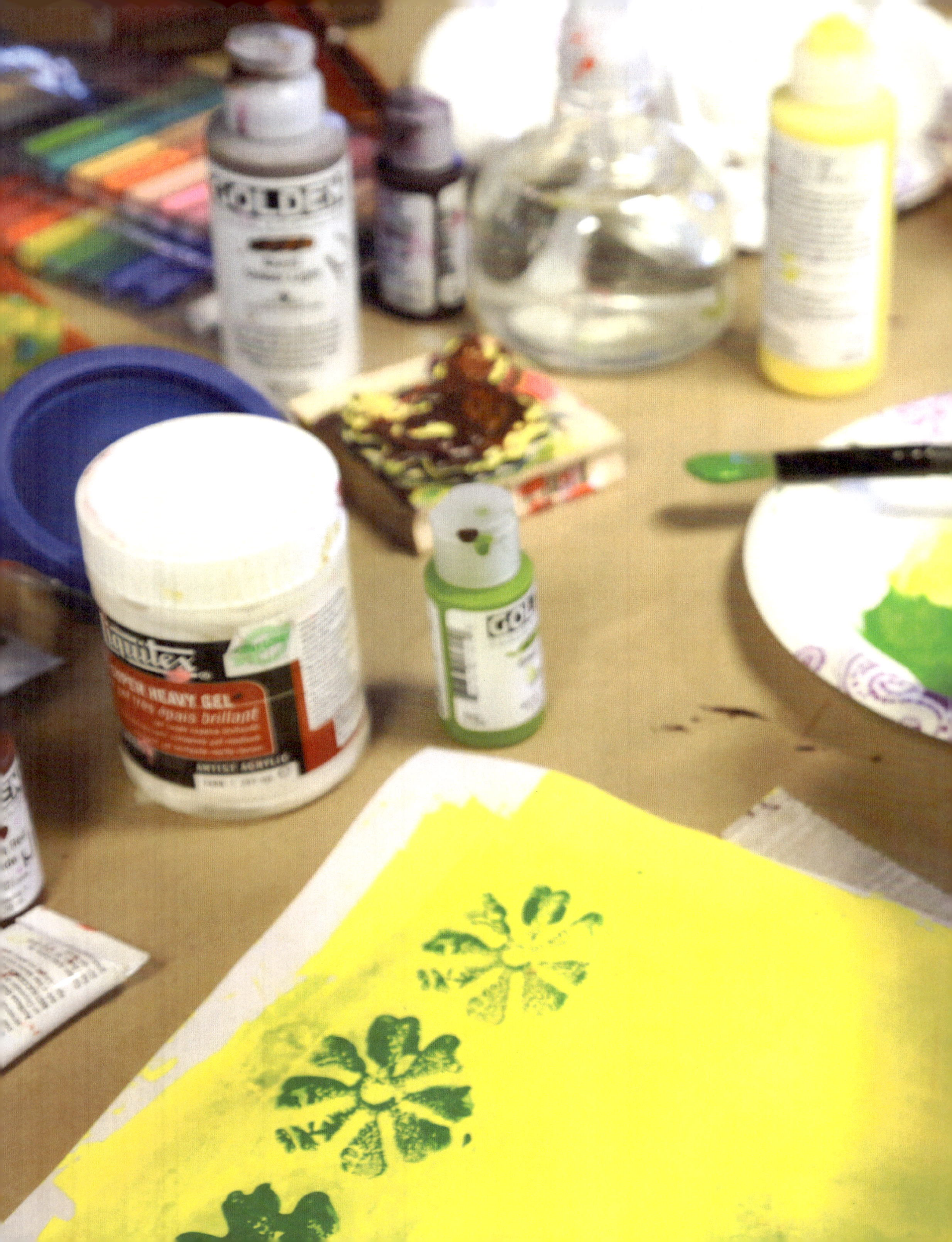

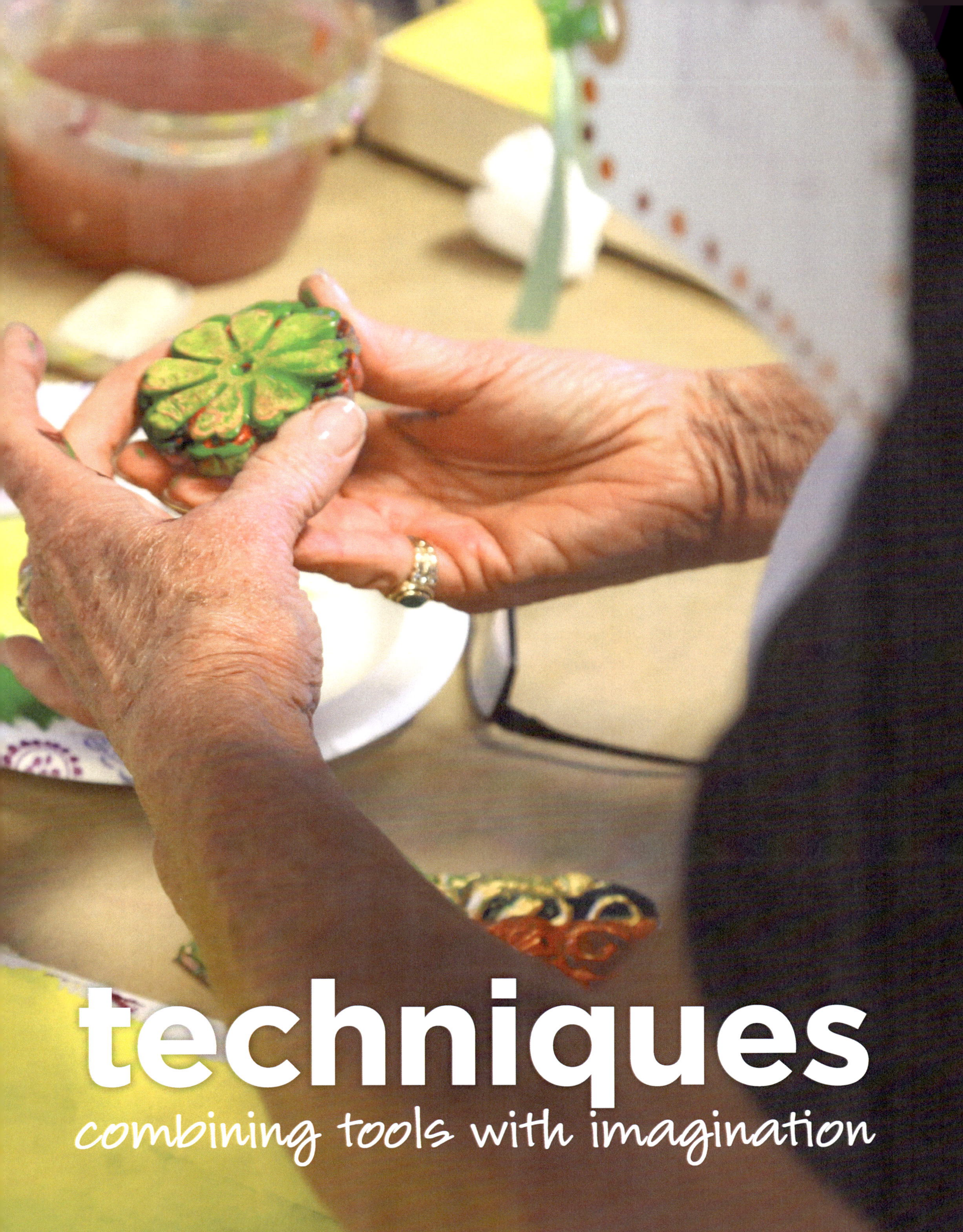
techniques
combining tools with imagination

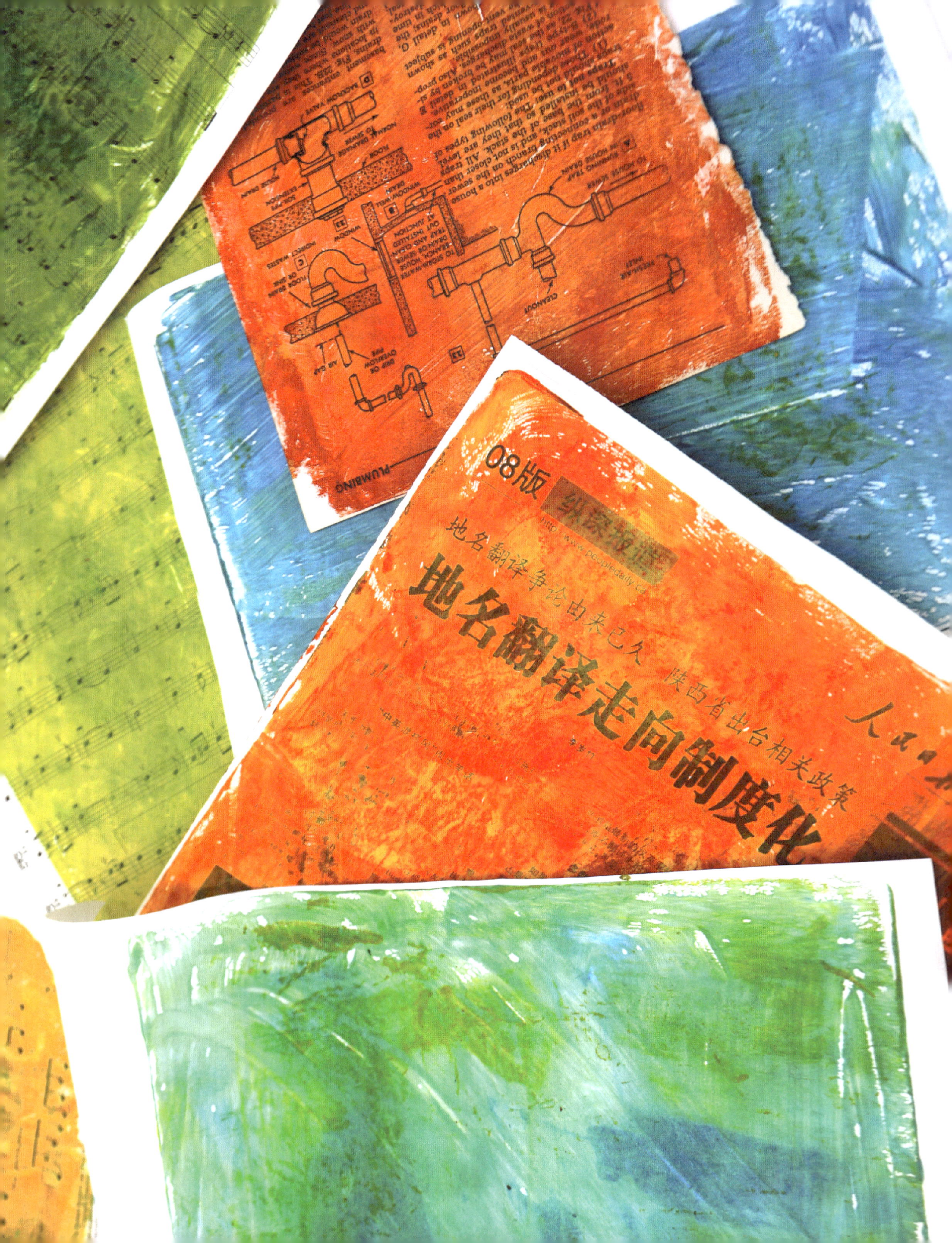
PLUMBING
08版
地名翻译争论由来已久
地名翻译走向制度化
陕西省出台相关政策

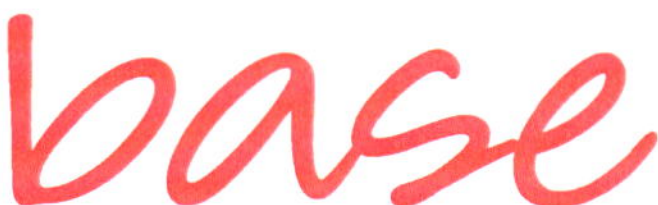

base
starting with light colored solids

I find, in fine art Gel printing, that starting with a light colored solid base is the way to go. I prefer not to have any high contrast white areas in my final prints, as I am hoping to achieve a painterly, fine art feeling. In order to eliminate the whites, without having to wash over the print post production, I always start with a solid base layer. I do not clean my plate between base layers, this process makes use of any residual paint on the plate from layer to layer. I call the leftover dried paint *the crust*. Your subsequent layers pick up *the crust* along with the newly applied paint -- creates unexpected and beautiful results.

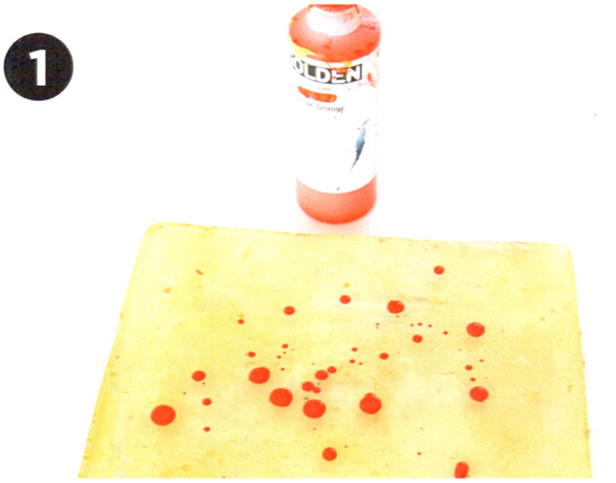

The brayer gives thin, even coverage for a few drops of paint applied directly to the plate.

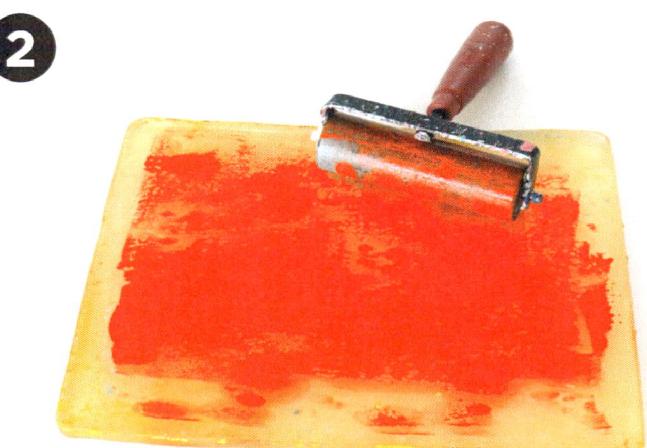

Roll the paint out to evenly cover the surface of the plate with the brayer.

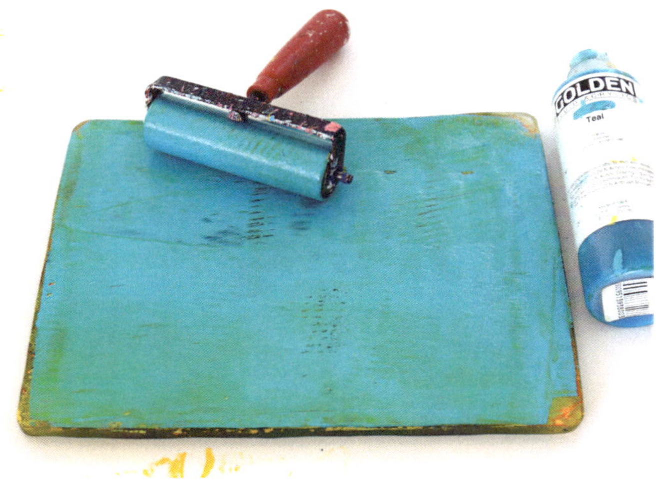

Start your printing process with a light colored solid.

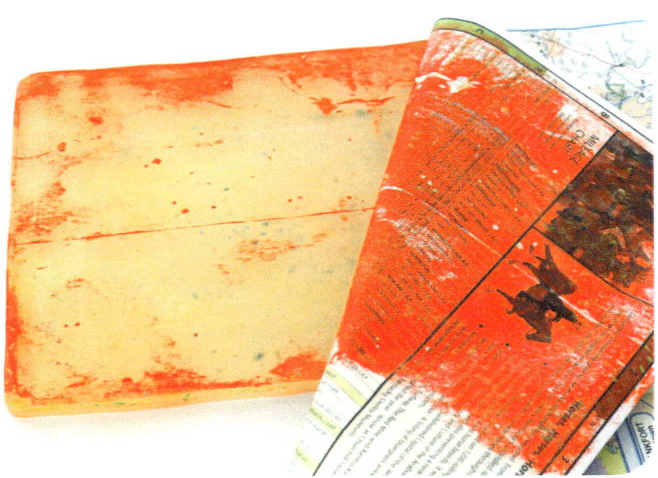

This will act as a base for subsequent, more complex layers

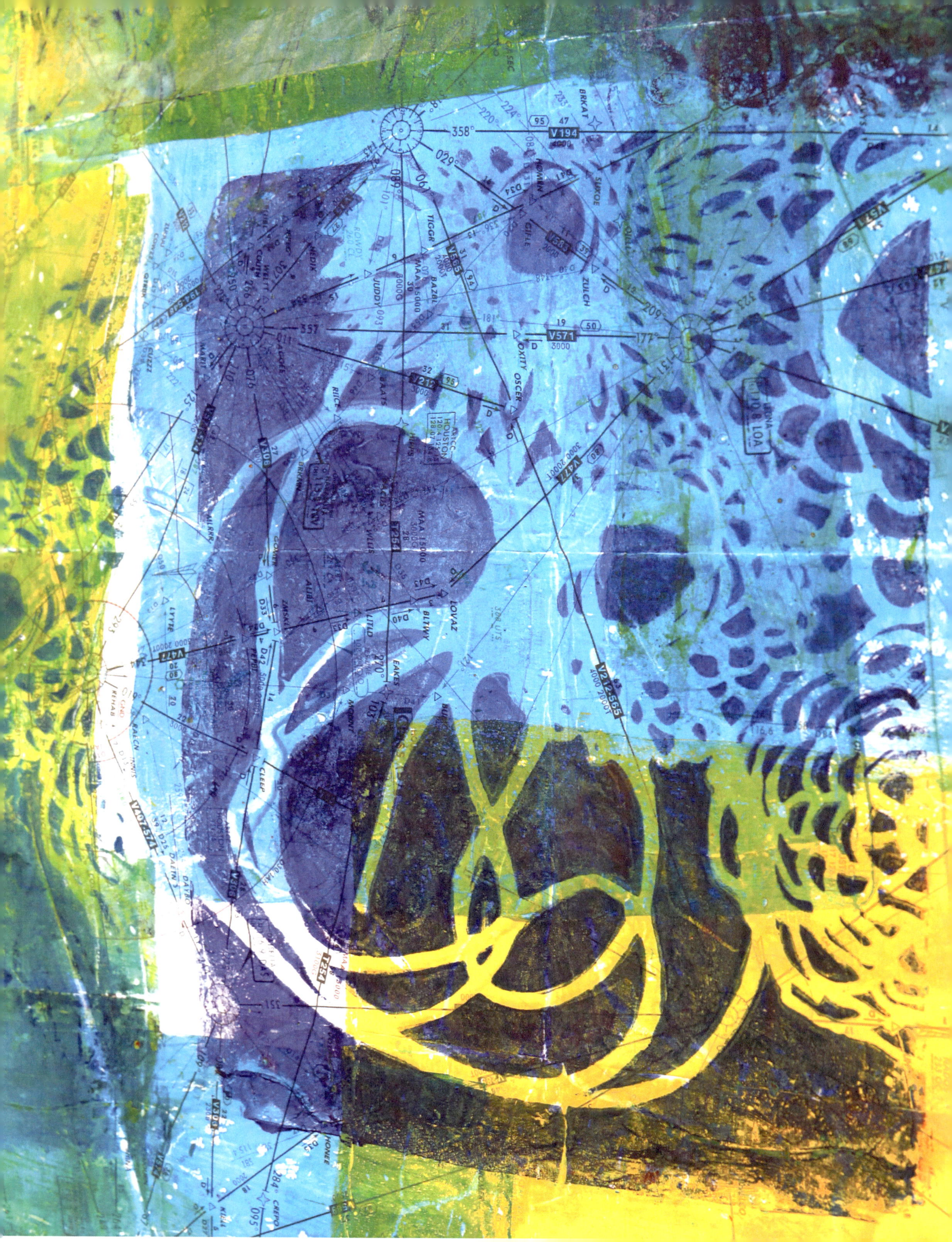

building layers

through translucency

Once you have your light colored base layer(s) printed on several small sheets of paper or an oversized sheet of paper, your goal is to start multiplying prints over and over with the techniques to follow in this book. Because fluid acrylics are translucent, every Gel printed layer you apply from here on out is going to show through and multiply with its predecessor. My typical rule of thumb is to combine a minimum of three layers in my Gel Prints, this creates rich papers for collage with lots and lots of depth. Varying the techniques of your layers creates even *more* visual interest. That being said, stencils tend to be the favorite technique of the Gel Press printing plate for my workshop students. My advice? *Be bold, branch out, try different things!*

The idea behind starting with a light colored base layer is that your prints don't include the *white* of the paper, which offers high contrast and can appear *busy*. High contrast can be distracting in collage papers, apple red should be layers of rich reds, intense oranges, deep yellows; adding white to this palette would be distracting.

I often multiply a print made using scraping tools over a print made with stencils, and then layer that print over one made with hand cut masks. This is the multi layered Gel print process I use for creating collage papers.

Keeping in mind my palette, I'll implement three or more colors (working from light to dark) that are analogous (next to one another) on the color wheel. I love the combination of blues and greens (cool colors) layered over each other through different techniques.

Every rule is meant to be broken! Experiment with combining opposites across the wheel as well.

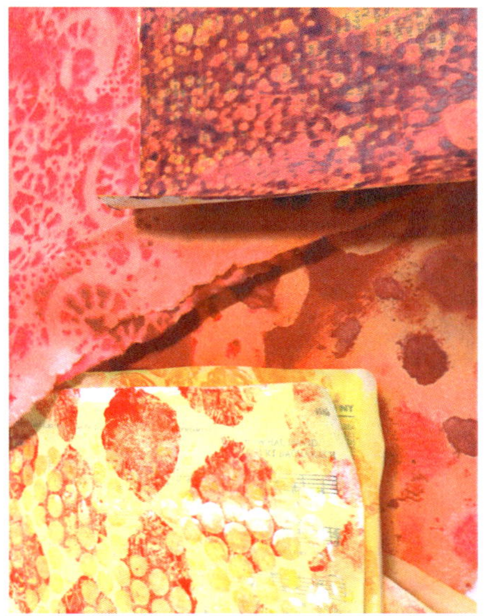

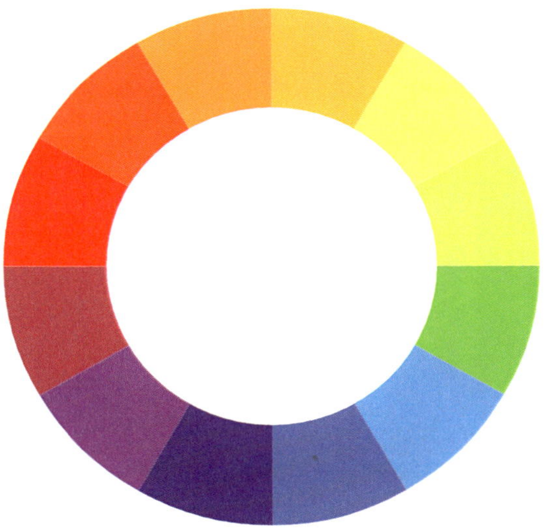

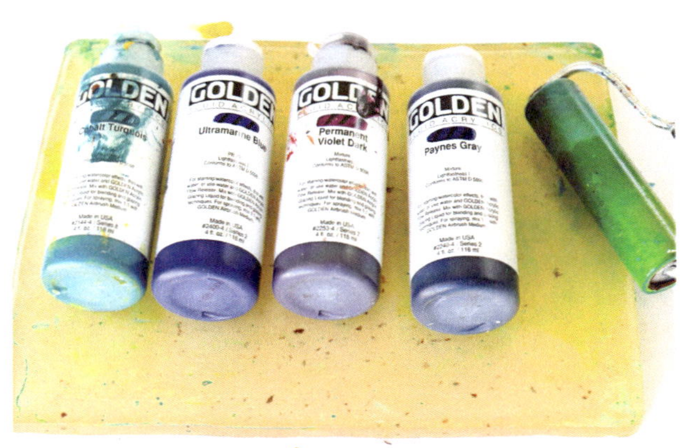

Making use of analogous colors.

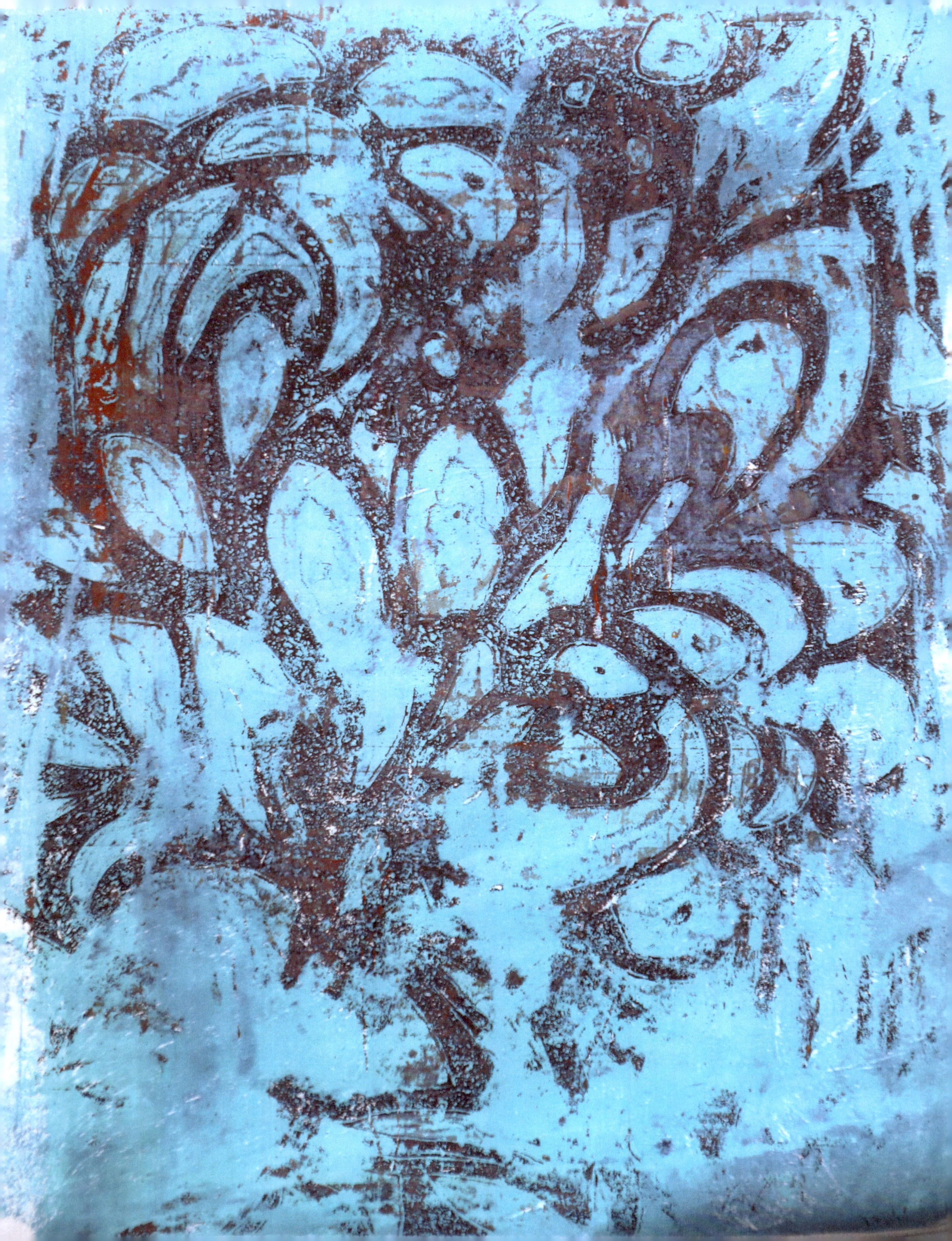

stencils

with ghost prints

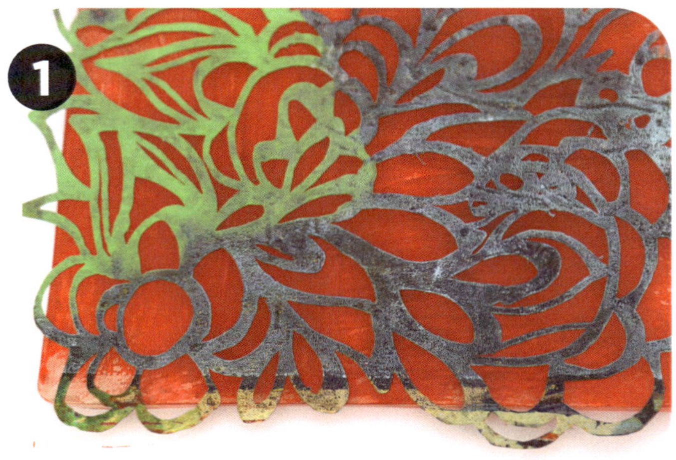

Lay the stencil over a thin layer of paint on the plate.

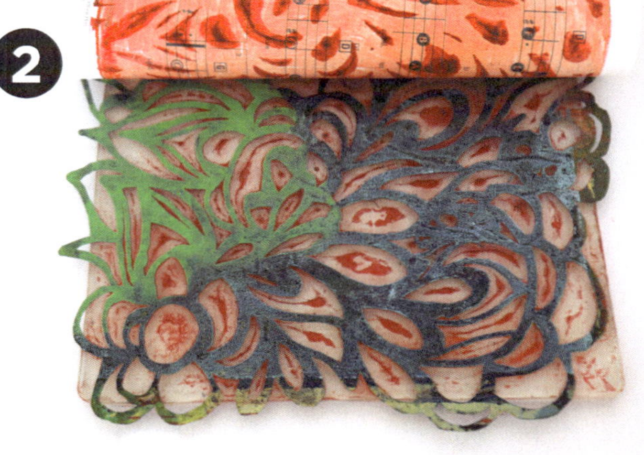

Press and pull a print from the plate

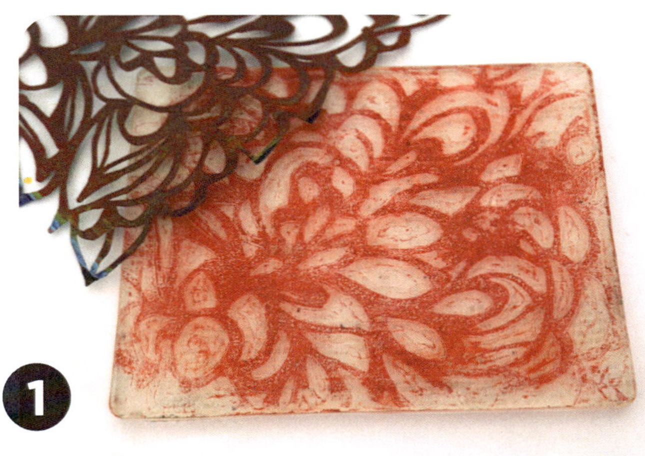

Paint left behind becomes the *ghost print*, or second print, after removing a stencil.

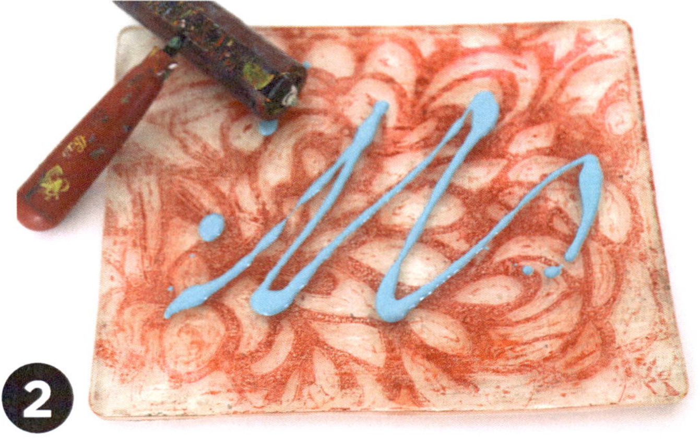

Add a thin layer of a lighter color paint over top of the dried *ghost* layer, pull the print of both layers together (see left).

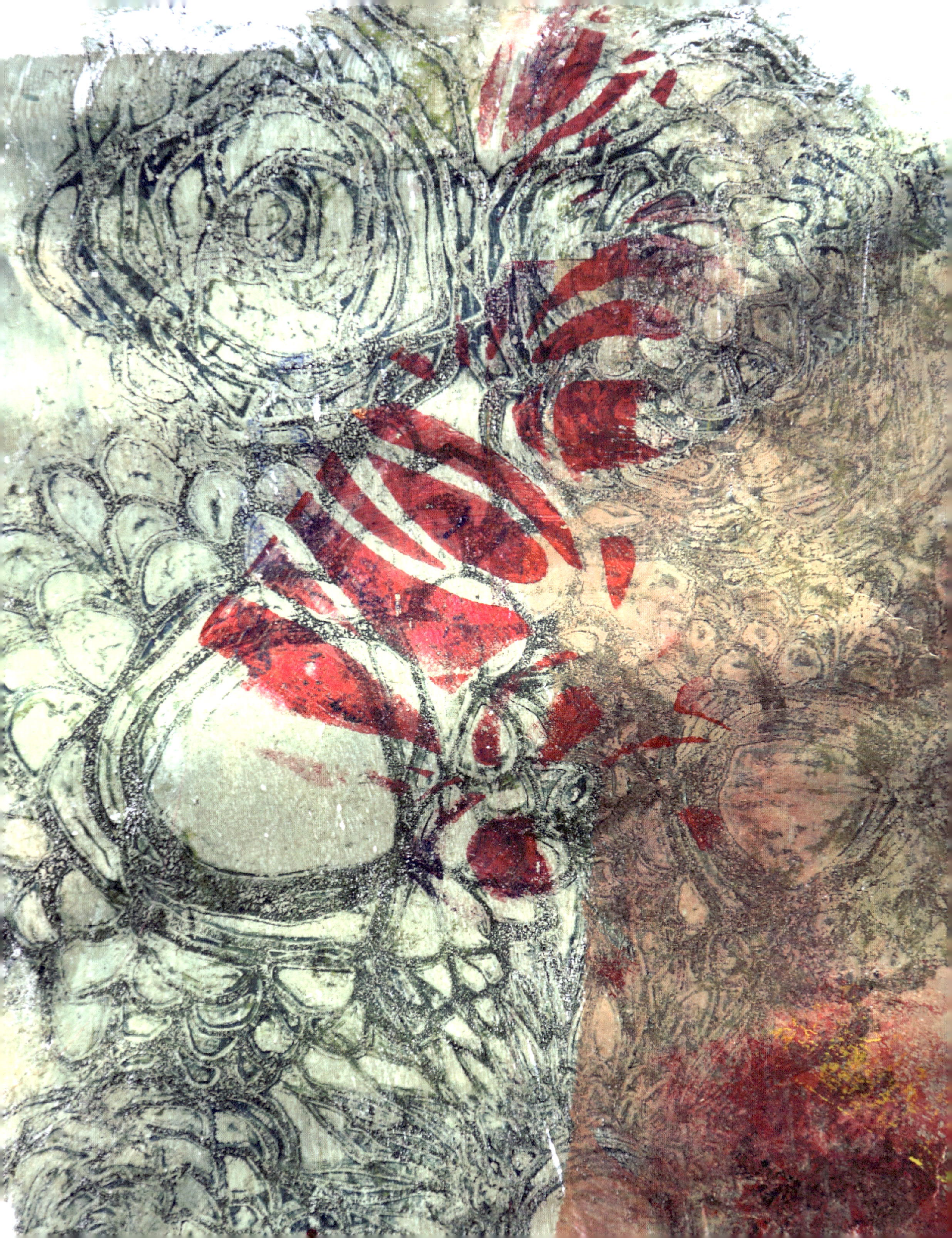

stencils
with ghost prints and watery washes

Layering ghost prints one over the next (working light to dark) offers rich, painterly printed paper. The more layering the better, when you are trying to achieve painterly, fine art prints. As a final step, try toning down the white areas with a wash of watered down color from your paint brush (left).

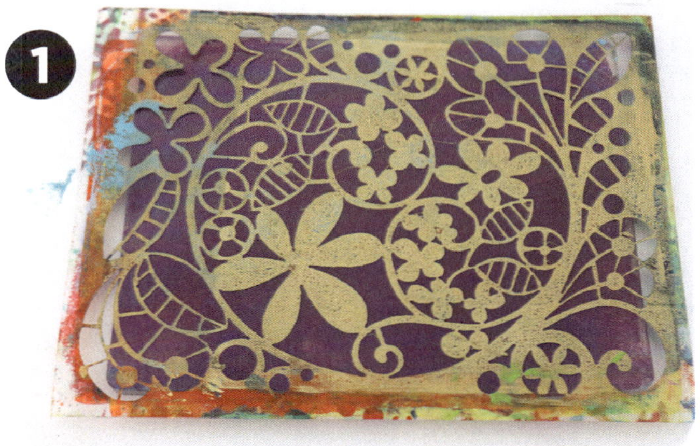

Purple paint on the plate, the stencil on top of the paint, ready to pull a print.

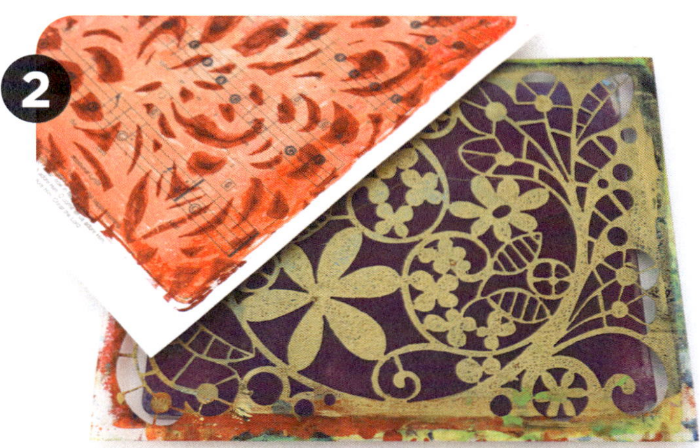

Pulling the purple print on top of an already established lighter stenciled print.

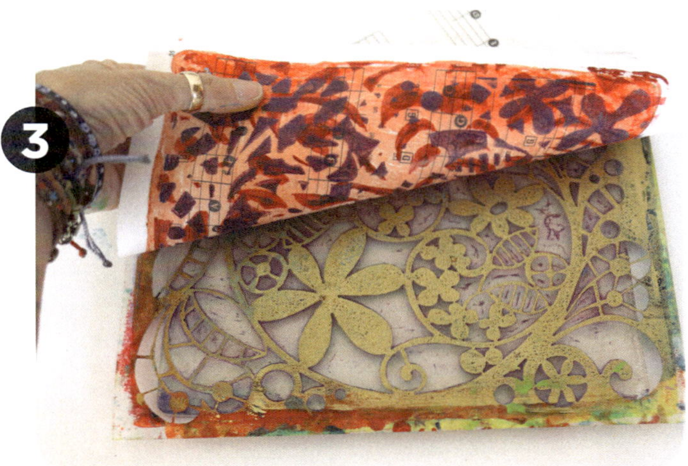

Trapped paint underneath stencils, small and large -- left behind from the first print.

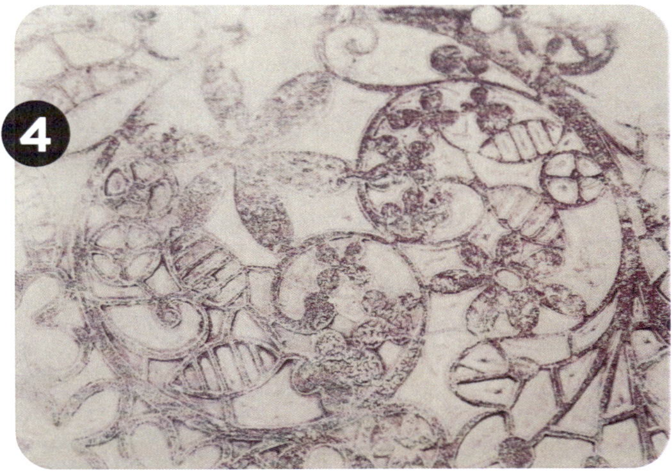

The ghost print on white will need to be toned down with a watery wash in order to subdue the whites.

When combining ghost prints on white paper, consider toning down the white areas by painting over the top with a watered down color wash. Take your fluid acrylics, add water, and use a soft bristled brush to paint over the dry Gel print. This makes for a different effect than working on top of a base layer. Experiment to see which effect you prefer. *Left: watery green and red washes over green ghost prints with red stenciling on top.*

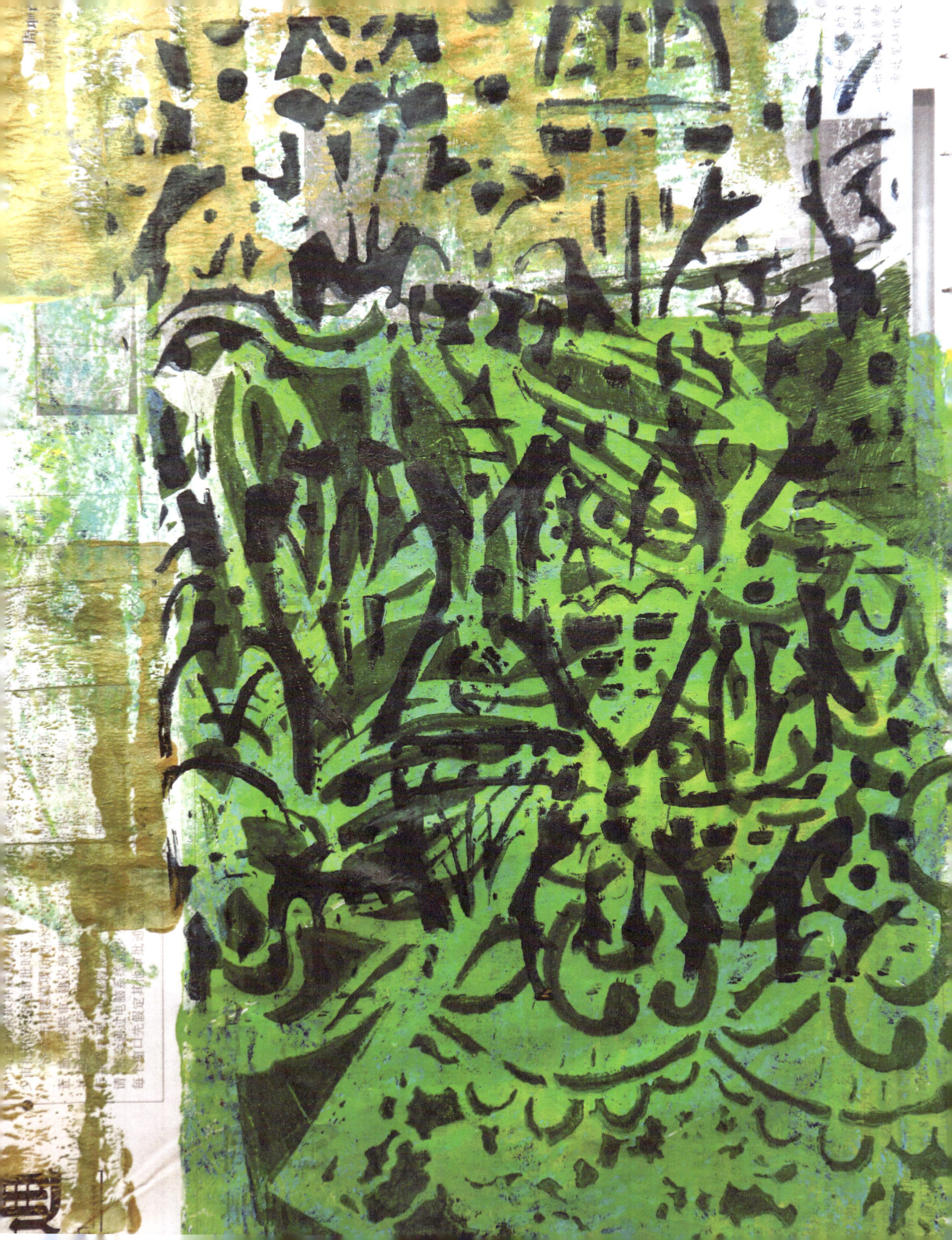

stencils
combining and layering

Layering stencil mask prints one over the next (working light to dark) offers rich, painterly printed paper. Combine stencils with elements such as leaves, string, and place mats for more diversity of patterning.

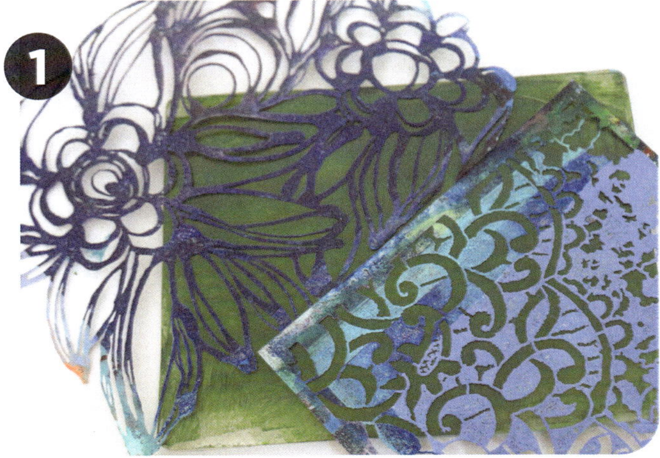

Combining two stencils on dark green paint.

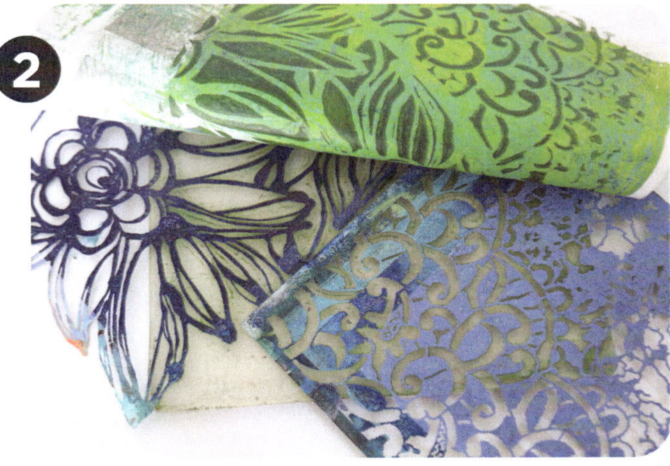

Pulling the multi stencil print on a light green solid.

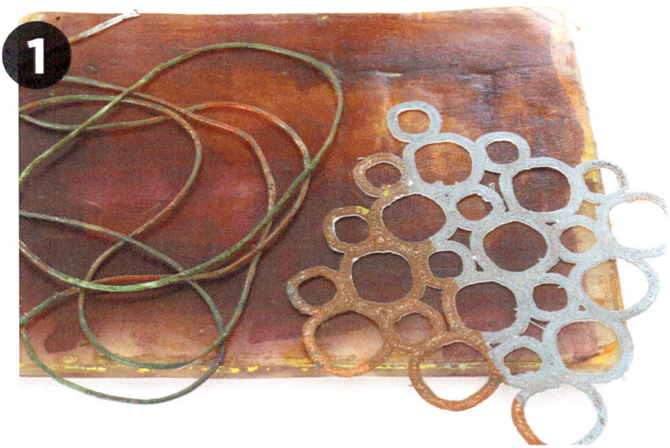

Combining a stencil with string
(or other found masking material) on one print.

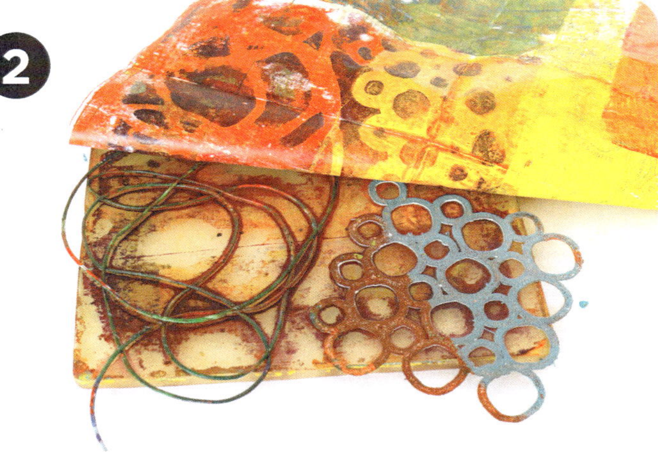

Pulling the print over a mixed solid base layer.

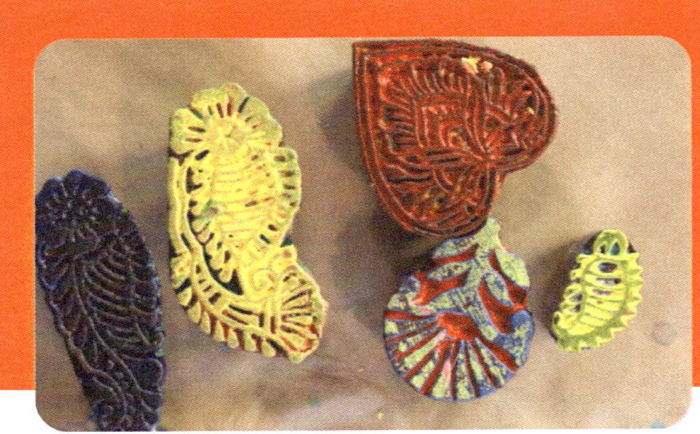

TIP

Batik stamps or *tjaps* work wonderfully when applied to remove paint from the Gel Press printing plate. You can find a wide range of batik tjaps on *Etsy.com*

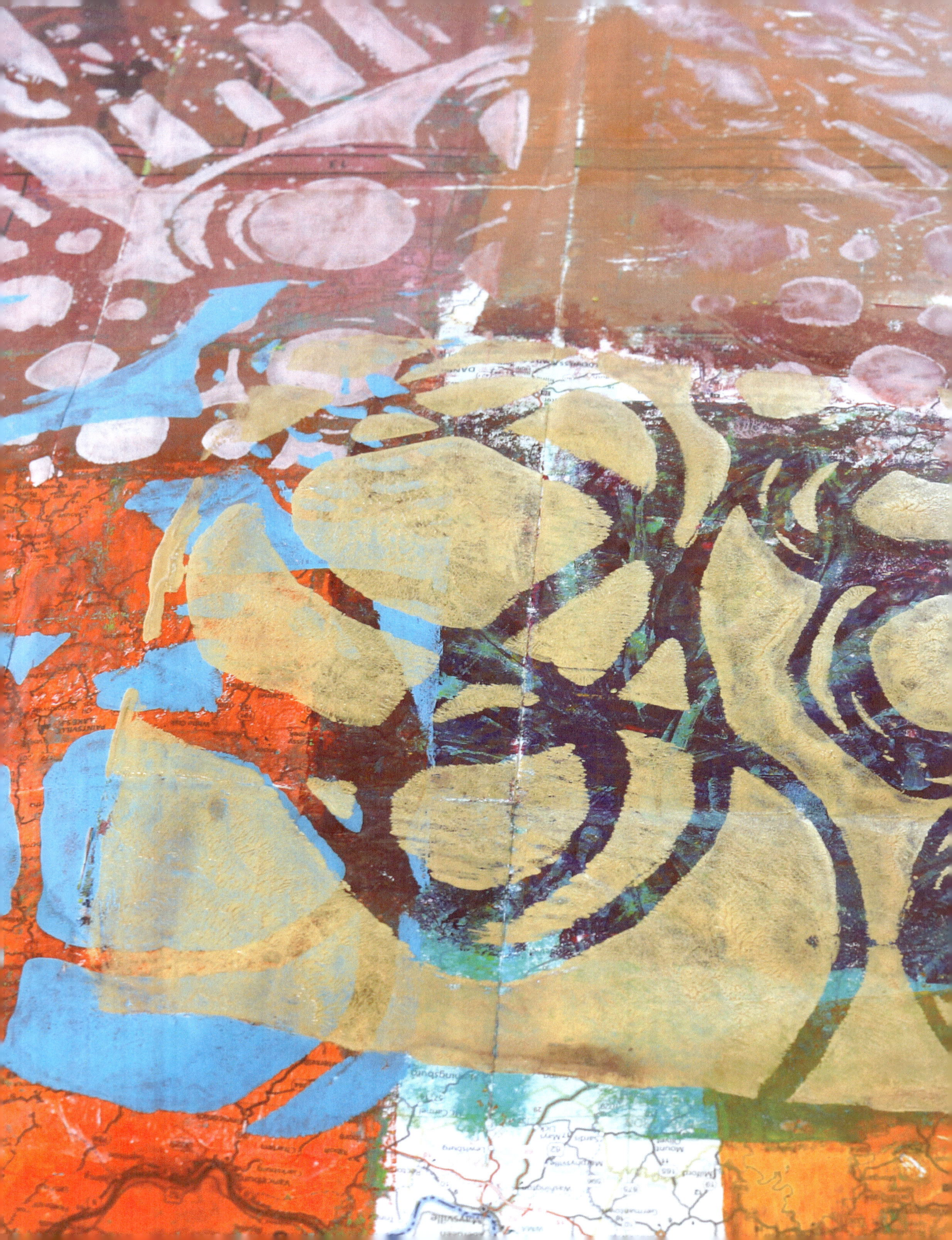

stencils
with gesso and opaque paints

You can take a print or prints that you feel are unsuccessful and give them new life with gesso. Gesso is opaque and when used with a stencil, allows only the area masked out by the stencil to show through. This makes your unsuccessful print act simply as a color field for the pattern of the stencil.

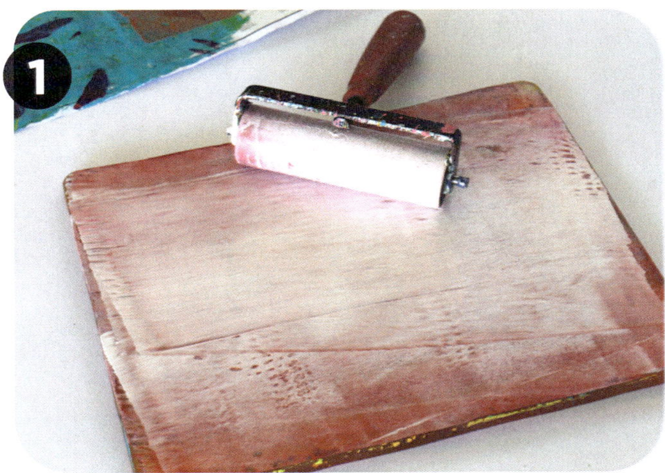

Roll out a thin layer of white gesso onto the plate.

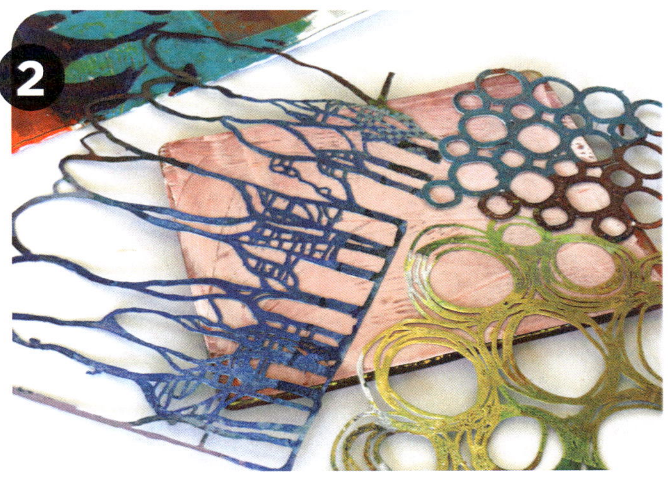

Lay stencils into the gesso.

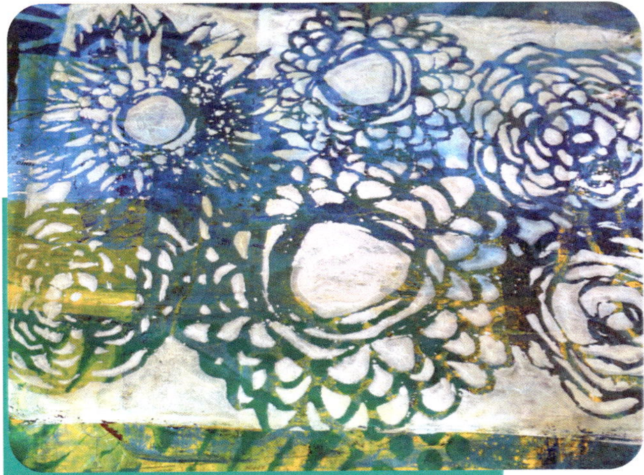

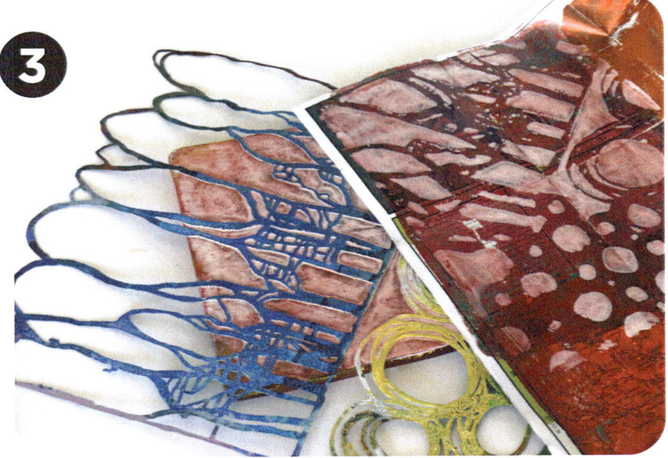

Use an unsuccessful print as the base layer for the gesso print, all will be masked out by the gesso except for the pattern of the stencil.

TIP

Both gesso and metallic fluid acrylic paints are opaque and offer you the opportunity to rescue unsuccessful or overly busy prints by masking over the top with a stencil.

Little, Brown & Co., 1923.

HOLDER, CHARLES FREDERICK. Louis Agassiz, His Life and Work. New York: G. P. Putnam's Sons, 1893.

HOLMES, OLIVER WENDELL. "The Human Wheel, Its Spokes and Felloes," Atlantic Monthly, May, 1863. Reprint published Boston: Ticknor & Fields, 1870.

HOMANS, J. E. Self-Propelled Vehicles. New York: Theo. Audel and Co., 1908.

HOWE, HENRY. Memoir of Most Eminent American Mechanics. New York: Derby & Jackson, 1858.

[illegible]. Men of Achievement. New York: Charles Scribner's Sons, 1894.

HUBERT, P. G. Men of Achievement, Inventors. New York: Charles Scribner's Sons, 1893.

HUNT, FREEMAN. Lives of American Merchants. New York: Derby and Jackson, [illegible].

[illegible], JOSEPH. The Story of the Bull [illegible]. Chicago: A. C. McClurg & [illegible].

[illegible], W. Triumphs and Wonders [illegible]. New York: [illegible] Century Co., [illegible].

[illegible] Leading [illegible]. New York: Henry Holt [illegible], 1910.

Illustrated Catalogue of the Centennial Exhibition, The. New York: John Fil[illegible] Trow, 1876.

INGRAM, J. S. The Centennial Exposition. Philadelphia: Hubbard Bros., 1876.

JACKSON, FREDERICK TURNER. The Frontier in American History. New York: Henry Holt & Co., Inc., 1920.

JAFFE, BERNARD. Crucibles. New York: Simon and Schuster, Inc., 1930.

JAFFE, BERNARD. Men of Science in America. New York: Simon and Schuster, Inc., 1946.

JAFFE, BERNARD. Outposts of Science. New York: Simon and Schuster, 1935.

JAMES, WILLIAM. "Louis Agassiz," Harvard Graduates' Magazine (Cambridge), June, 1897.

JENSEN, PAUL. The Fireside Book of Flying Stories. New York: Simon and Schuster, 1951.

JONES, [illegible] D. The American Portrait Gallery. New York: Henry Miller, 1869.

[illegible], MATTHEW. The Robber Barons. New York: Harcourt, Brace & Co., [illegible].

[illegible], NATHAN. Walter Hunt, American Inventor. New York: 1935.

[illegible], D. H. and KAHN, ALFRED E. Big Business in a Competitive Society. (New York: Fortune Magazine) Feb[illegible].

KELLY, FRED C. The Wright Brothers. New York: Harcourt, Brace & Co., 1943.

KIRKLAND, EDWARD C. A History of American Economic Life. New York: F. S. Crofts and Co., 1934.

Knight's American Mechanical Dictionary. New York: Hurd & Houghton, 187[illegible].

[illegible] Textile Industries of [illegible]. SMITH & OVERTON. Boston: [illegible]. H. Lamb, 1916[illegible].

LAMB, R. W. Henry Ford's Own Story. New York: Ellis O. Jones, 1917.

LANGLEY, SAMUEL PIERPONT. Memoir on [illegible] Flight. 2 vols. C. H. MANLY. Washington: Smithsonian Institution, 1911.

LANGMUIR, IRVING. Phenomena, Atoms and Molecules. New York: Philosophical Library, 1950.

LARRABEE, DIONYS. The Museum of [illegible] and Art. London: Walton & M[illegible], 1856.

LESLIE, FRANK. Historical Register of the United States Centennial Exposition. New York: Frank Leslie, [illegible].

LESLIE, FRANK. Pictorial History [illegible]. New York: Frank Leslie's [illegible].

[illegible], LAWRENCE P. The Electrician. [illegible] Annual Magazine (New York), July, 1951.

[illegible], A. A. Life, Letters and Works of Louis Agassiz. New York: The Macmillan Co., 1896.

MICHELSON, A. A. Light Waves and Their Uses. Chicago: University of Chicago Press, 1903.

MICHELSON, A. A. Studies in Optics. Chicago: University of Chicago Press, 1927.

MILLIKAN, R. A. The Autobiography of [illegible]. New York: Prentice-Hall, Inc., 1950.

[illegible] The Illustrated [illegible]. Boston: The Macmillan Co., 1952.

MONTROSS, LYNN. War Through the Ages. New York: Harper & Bros., 1944.

MORISON, SAMUEL ELIOT. The Maritime History of Massachusetts. Boston: Houghton, Mifflin Co., 1921.

MORRIS, EDMUND. Derrick and Drill. New York: James Miller, 186[illegible].

MORSE, SAMUEL F. B. His Letters and Journals. E. LIND MORSE, ed. Boston: Houghton, Mifflin Co., 1914.

[illegible], EDWARD A. Anonymous Authorship. New York: Brentano's, 1929.

HAVEN: Yale University Press [illegible].

RIESMAN, DAVID. The Lonely Crowd. New Haven: Yale University Press, 1950.

ROBINSON, WILLIAM MORRISON, JR. The Confederate Privateers. New Haven: Yale University Press, 1928.

ROE, JOSEPH WICKHAM. English and American Tool Builders. New Haven: Yale University Press, 1916.

[illegible] Interchangeable [illegible].

[illegible] Hopkins [illegible] 1902.

RUKEYSER, MURIEL. Willard Gibbs. New York: Doubleday, Doran & Co., 1942.

RUMFORD, COUNT. Collected Works of. Boston: American Academy of Arts and Sciences, [illegible].

ST. MARTIN, ALEXIS. Four Letters [illegible]. Ann Arbor: William L. Clements Library, 1937.

St. Nicholas, Vol. XI, part 2. New York: The Century Co., 1884.

SCHLUETER, ROBERT E. "A Short Biographical Sketch of Dr. William Beaumont." Address before medical staff and resi[illegible].

SLOSSON, [illegible]. The Book of the [illegible]. New York: D. Appleton & Co., 1905.

SMITH, [illegible]. Lives of [illegible]. [illegible]: J. Murray, [illegible].

SMITH, [illegible]. Chemistry in [illegible]. New York: D. Appleton & Co., [illegible].

SMITH, [illegible]. Chemistry in Old Philadelphia. Philadelphia: J. B. Lippincott Co., [illegible].

SMITH, [illegible]. Priestly in America. Philadelphia: Blakiston, 1920.

[illegible] The Elements [illegible].

[illegible]. Annapolis: U. S. Naval Institute, 1922.

[illegible] London and Edinburgh Philosophical Magazine. London: [illegible] Taylor, June, 1840.

[illegible], CARLTON. The American Leonardo, a Life of Samuel [illegible] Morse. New York: Alfred A. Knopf, 1943.

[illegible], MATTHEW. Information and Directions [illegible] Company Wind and Current Charts [illegible].

[illegible] MATTHEW. [illegible]. New York: Collins, Keese & Co., 1839.

McKAY, [illegible]. Famous Sailing [illegible]. 1850[illegible].

[illegible] Life of [illegible]. Henderson [illegible], 1850[illegible].

RENWICK, [illegible]. Life of [illegible]. New York: Harper [illegible].

[illegible] New York: Henry Holt [illegible].

[illegible] Catalogue of the Centennial Exhibition [illegible]. New York: Prentice [illegible].

of Fortune and R[illegible]. New York: Prentice [illegible].

United States Centennial Commission, International Exhibition [illegible] Catalogue. New York: [illegible] Co., 1876.

United States Centennial Commission, International Exhibition [illegible] Reports and Awards, The. Philadelphia: J. B. Lippincott [illegible].

[illegible], The American [illegible] Magnetic Telegraph. Washington: Gideon, 1845.

VAN DOREN, CARL. Benjamin Franklin. New York: Viking Press, [illegible].

VERY, EDWARD W. Navies of the World. New York: John Wiley & Sons, 1880.

WIENER, NORBERT. The Human Use of Human Beings. Boston: Houghton, Mifflin Co., 1950.

WESTCOTT, THOMPSON. Centennial Portfolio. Philadelphia: Thomas Hunter, 1876.

WESTCOTT, THOMPSON. Life of John Fitch. Philadelphia: J. B. Lippincott, 1857.

[illegible], WILLIAM ALLEN. [illegible]. New York: Macmillan [illegible].

[illegible]. New York: American [illegible] Review, 1897.

WILSON, H. W. Ironclads in Action. London: Sampson Low, et al., 1896.

WILSON, J. M. Masterpieces of the Centennial International Exhibition. 3 vols. Philadelphia: Gebbie & Barrie, 1876.

Wireless Age, New York: Marconi Publishing Co., 1914.

WISTER, OWEN. The Virginian. Illus. Fred Remington. New York: Harper Brothers, 1900.

WOLF, RALPH F. India Rubber Man. Caldwell, Idaho: Caxton Printers, Ltd., 1939.

WRIGHT, ORVILLE. How We Invented the Airplane. FRED C. KELLY, ed. New York: David McKay Co., Inc., 1953.

masks
making and combining

Masks can be as simple as cutting strips and layering the prints with opposite directions to create a basket weave. You do not have to make complex shapes when your goal in to create a painterly Gel print, all you need to create is a texture or pattern. You may use palette paper for this effect, be sure to place the shiny side of the paper down onto the painted plate.

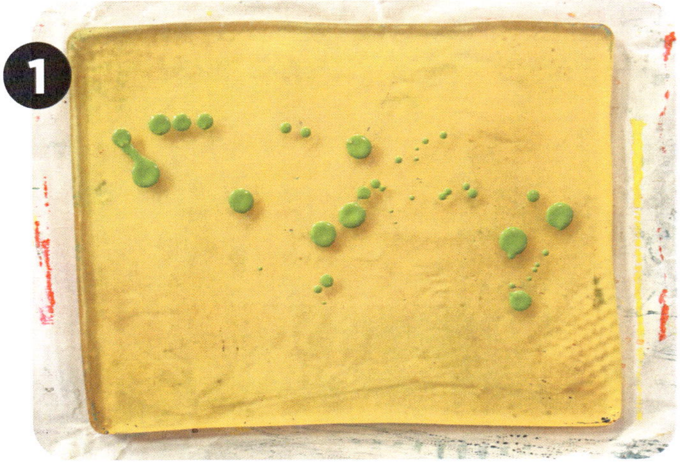

Start with a thin layer of light green paint.

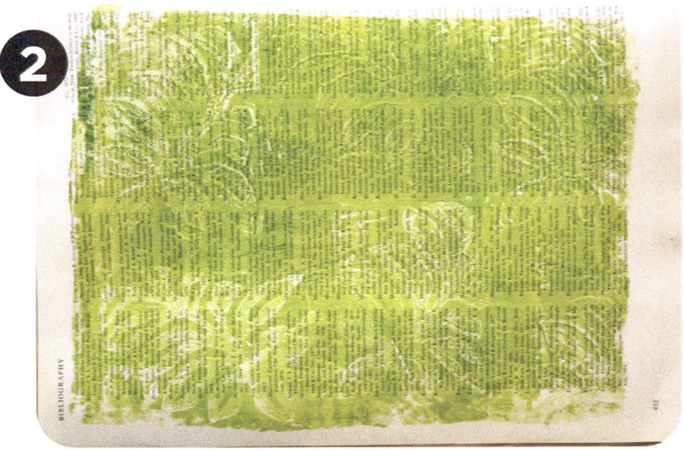

Create a subtle base layer for the masks,
here I am using a recycled book page.

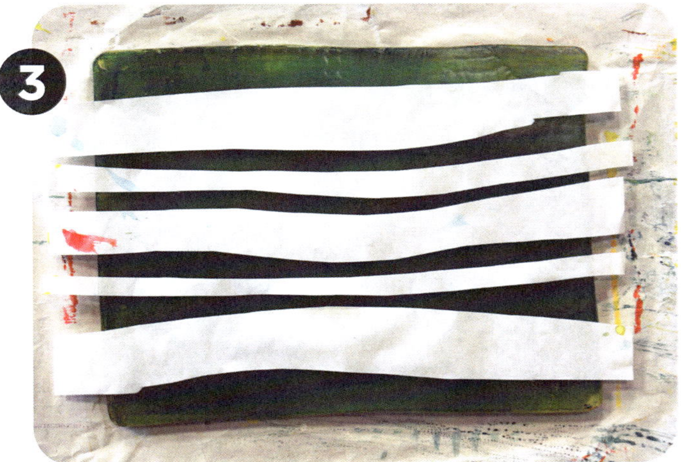

Lay strips of palette paper horizontally and
pull a print over the light green print.

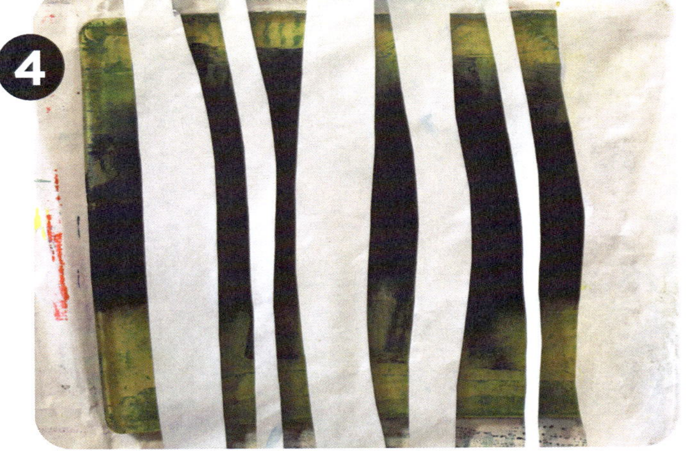

Lay strips of palette paper vertically and
pull a second print over the same paper.

TIP

When you want to clean your Gel Press printing plate, there's only one efficient way to do it. Let all the paint dry, take **heavy duty** clear packing tape strips and cover the entire plate, edges included. Burnish, or rub the tape very firmly with your hands so that it makes good contact. Peel back the tape to reveal a clean plate! The tackiness of the tape removes all the paint, it simply peels off.

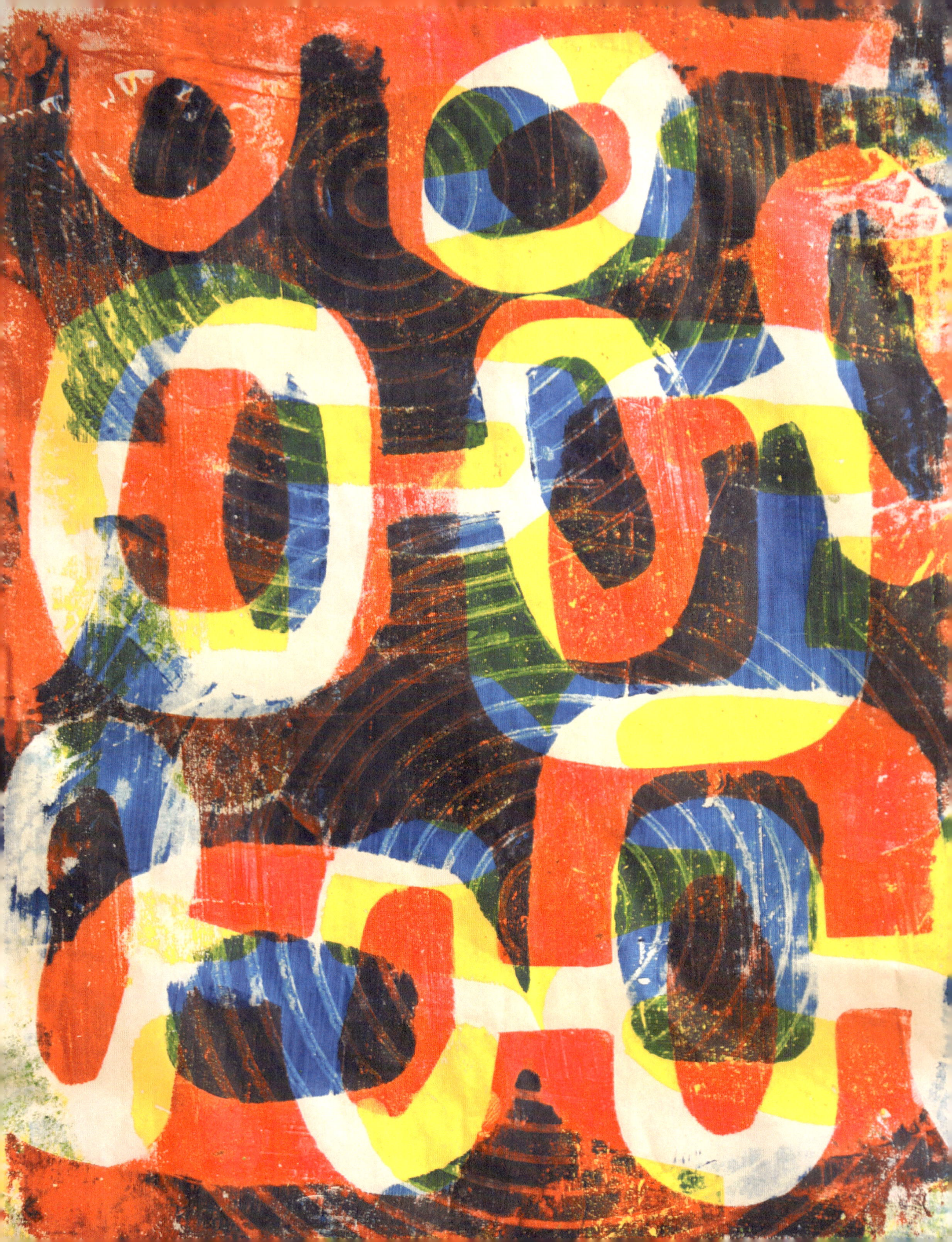

masks
unique designs

Masks can be as simple as cutting strips of shapes and layering the prints with opposite directions. You do not have to make complex shapes when your goal in to create a painterly Gel print, all you need to create is a texture or pattern. You may use Tyvek paper for this effect, which is the material that FedEx envelopes, and Priority Mail envelopes from the Post Office are made from.

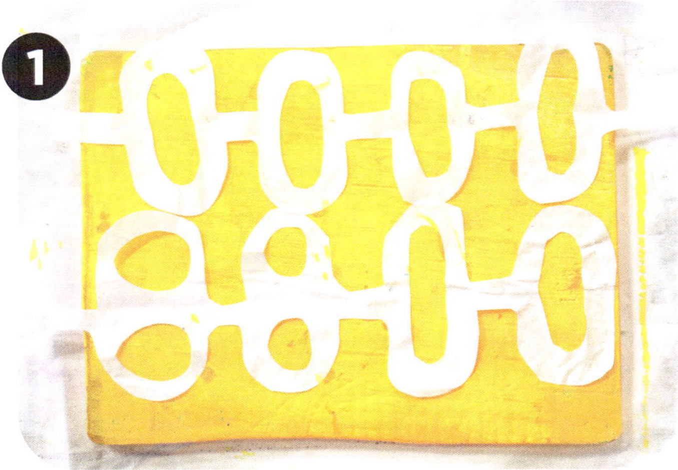

1. Lay the masks into the wet paint and pull the first layer print, this time onto white paper.

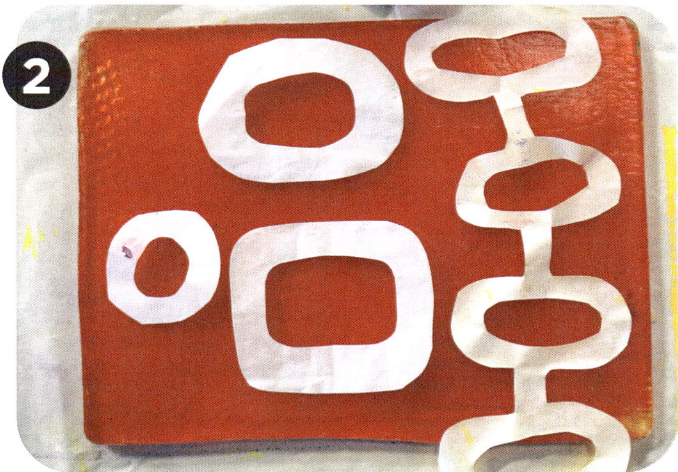

2. Switch the position of the masks and use a slightly darker paint color on the plate.

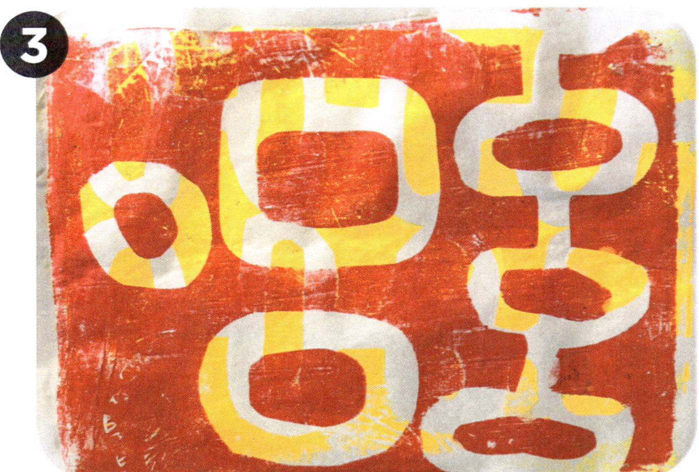

3. Print the second print directly on top of the first.

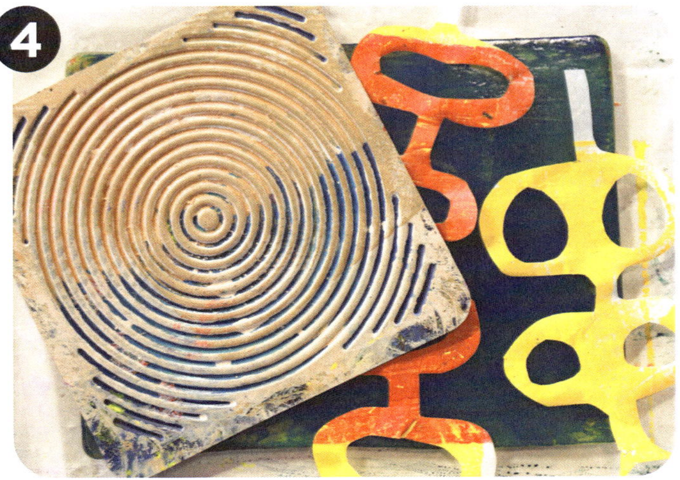

4. Press and remove a texture plate into the final dark paint layer to remove a subtle pattern in the paint.

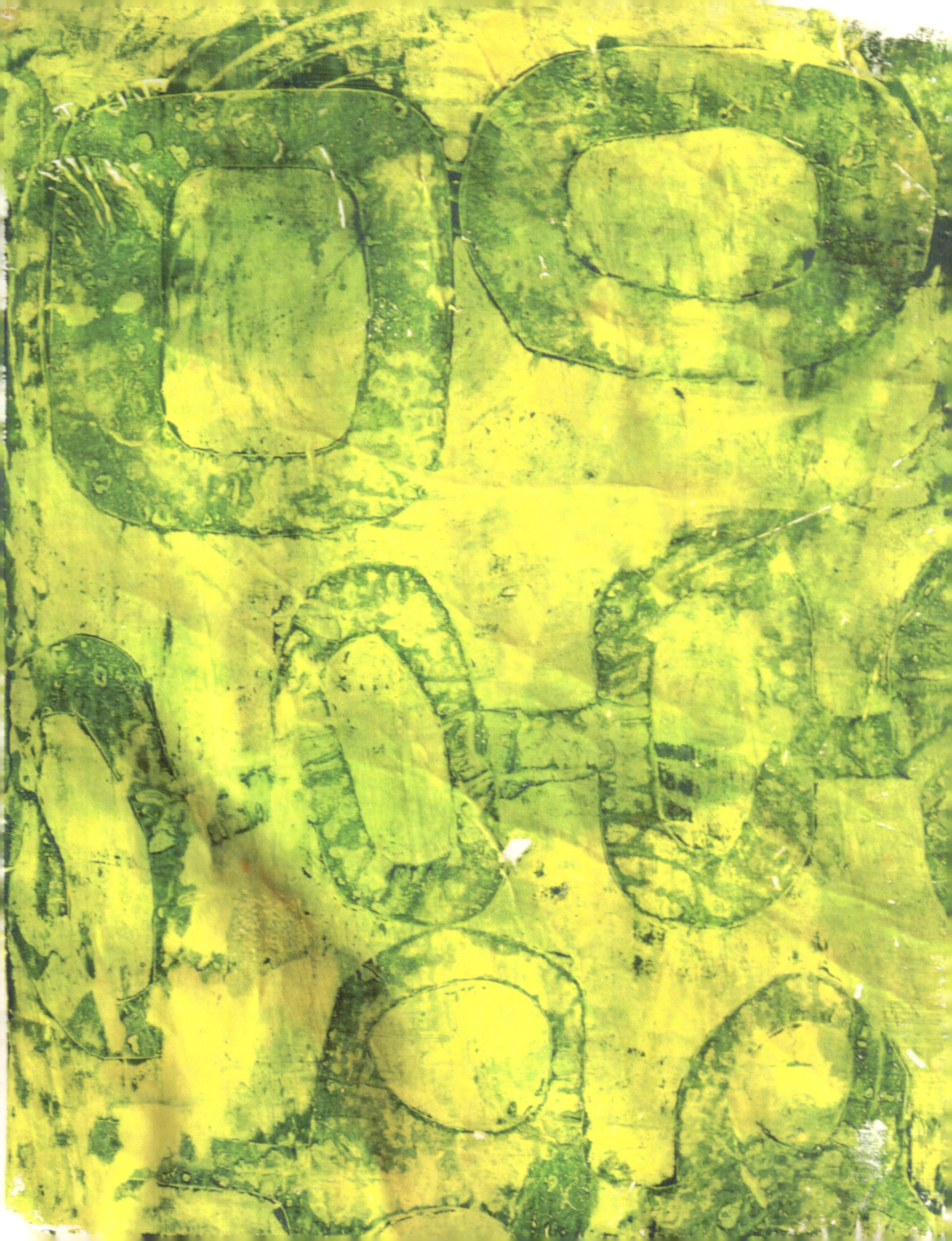

masks
ghost printing

Remember that the trapped paint underneath the mask makes for lovely *ghost* prints. Each time you peel the mask off the plate, take advantage of that trapped paint for a second print, typically over a light colored solid.

Pull a light yellow sheet base layer to print the *ghost print* on top of.

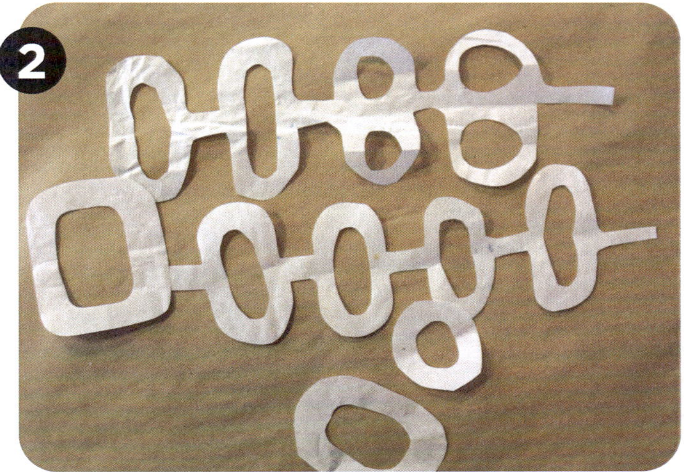

Cut shapes out of Tyvek. This is the material that Federal Express envelopes are made from.

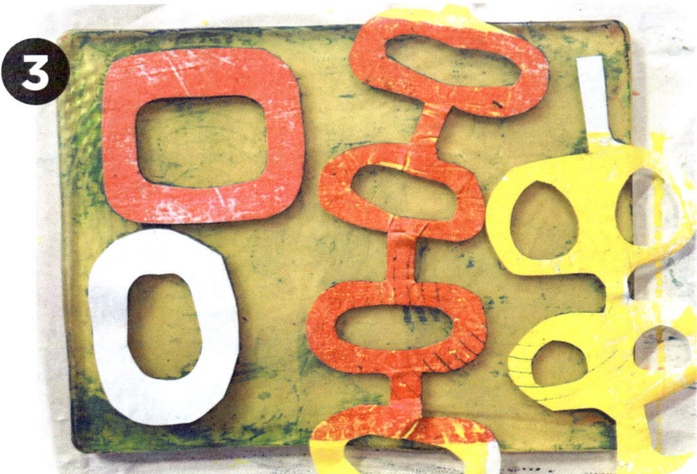

Paint is trapped under the masks after the first print is pulled and set aside.

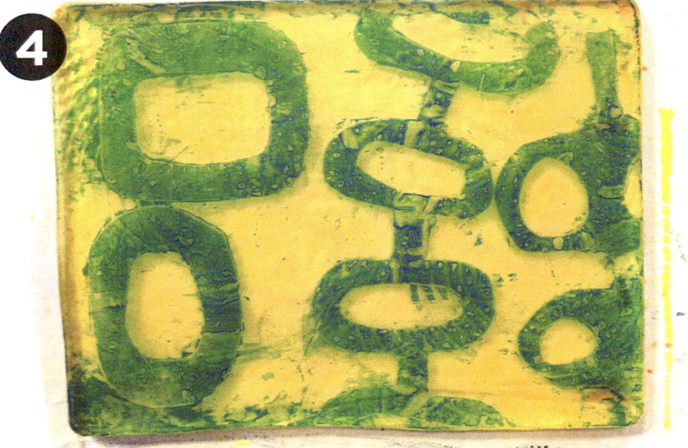

Gently remove the Tyvek shapes to reveal the trapped paint underneath.

Left: The ghost print of green from above is printed over the prepared yellow solid.

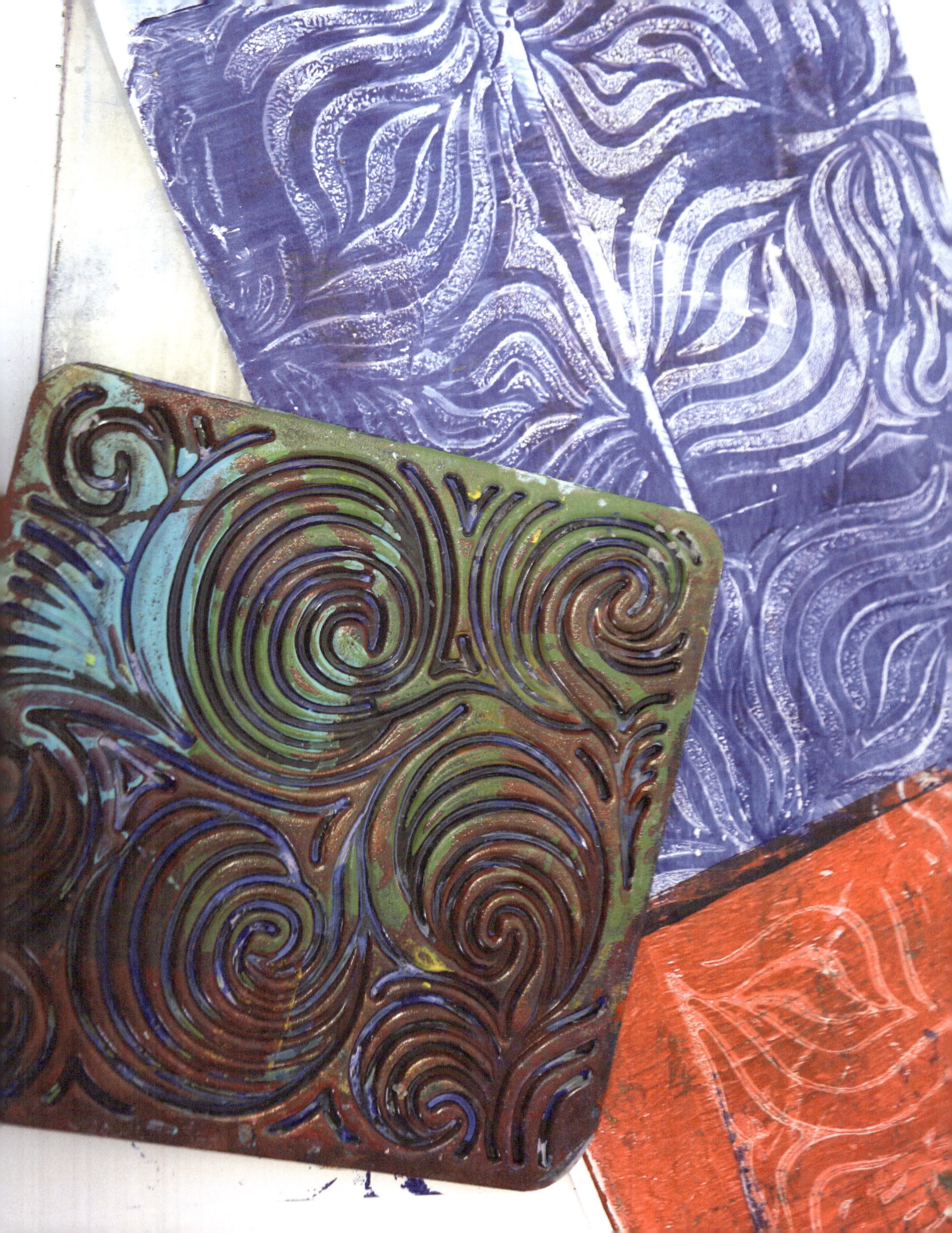

texture

plastic rubbing plates

There are many ways to apply texture to Gel Prints, commercially produced texture plates being just the beginning. Other elements that can be used include, the bottoms of shoes, the circle end of a paper towel roll, potato mashing tools, yoga mats, needle point mesh... the possibilities are endless. Look around you and start thinking about the everyday items in your life and how they would work when pressed into paint on the Gel Press printing plate. It's a whole new world.

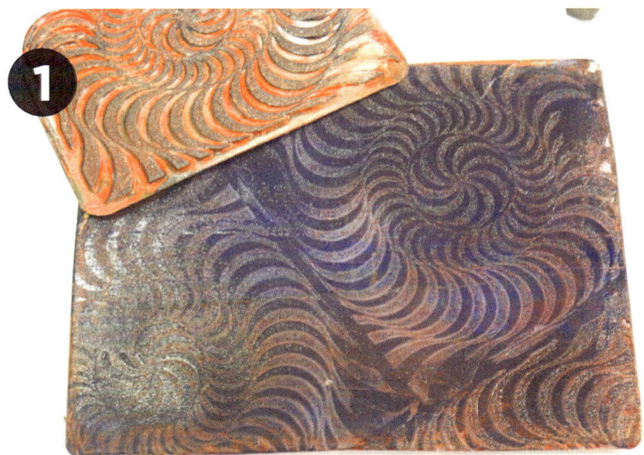

Press a clean, dry rubbing plate into a wet layer of paint to create a pattern by removing paint.

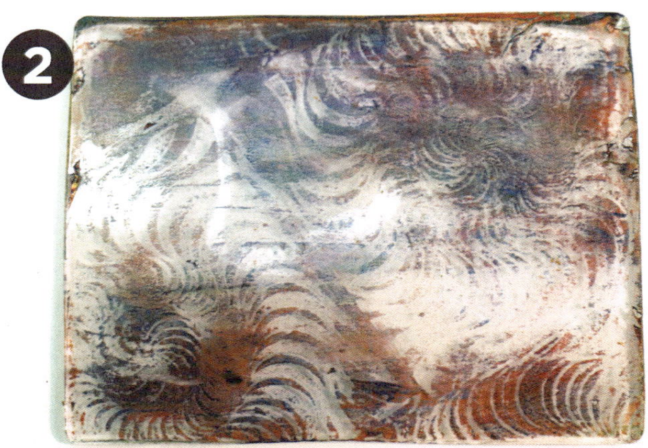

After the first print of the rubbing plate, let the residual paint dry on the plate.

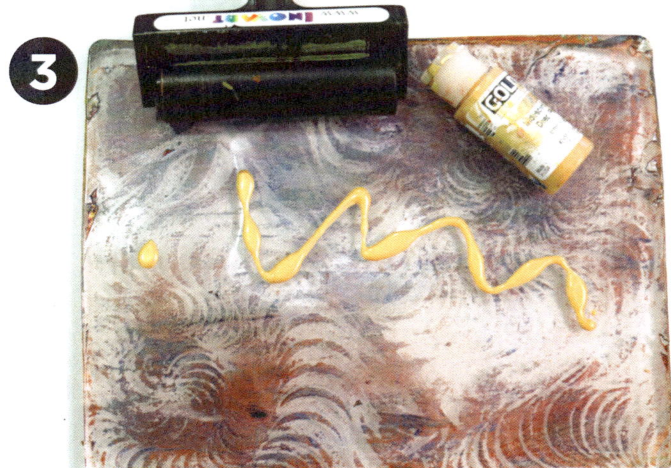

Apply a gold metallic over the residual paint.

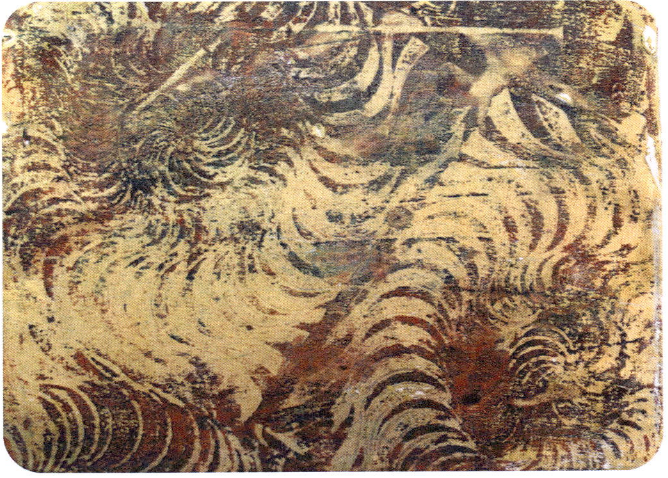

The gold metallic paint and the residual paint are pulled together to create one print, as shown here.

Left: A rubbing plate was used to remove paint and the print was pulled over white rice paper.

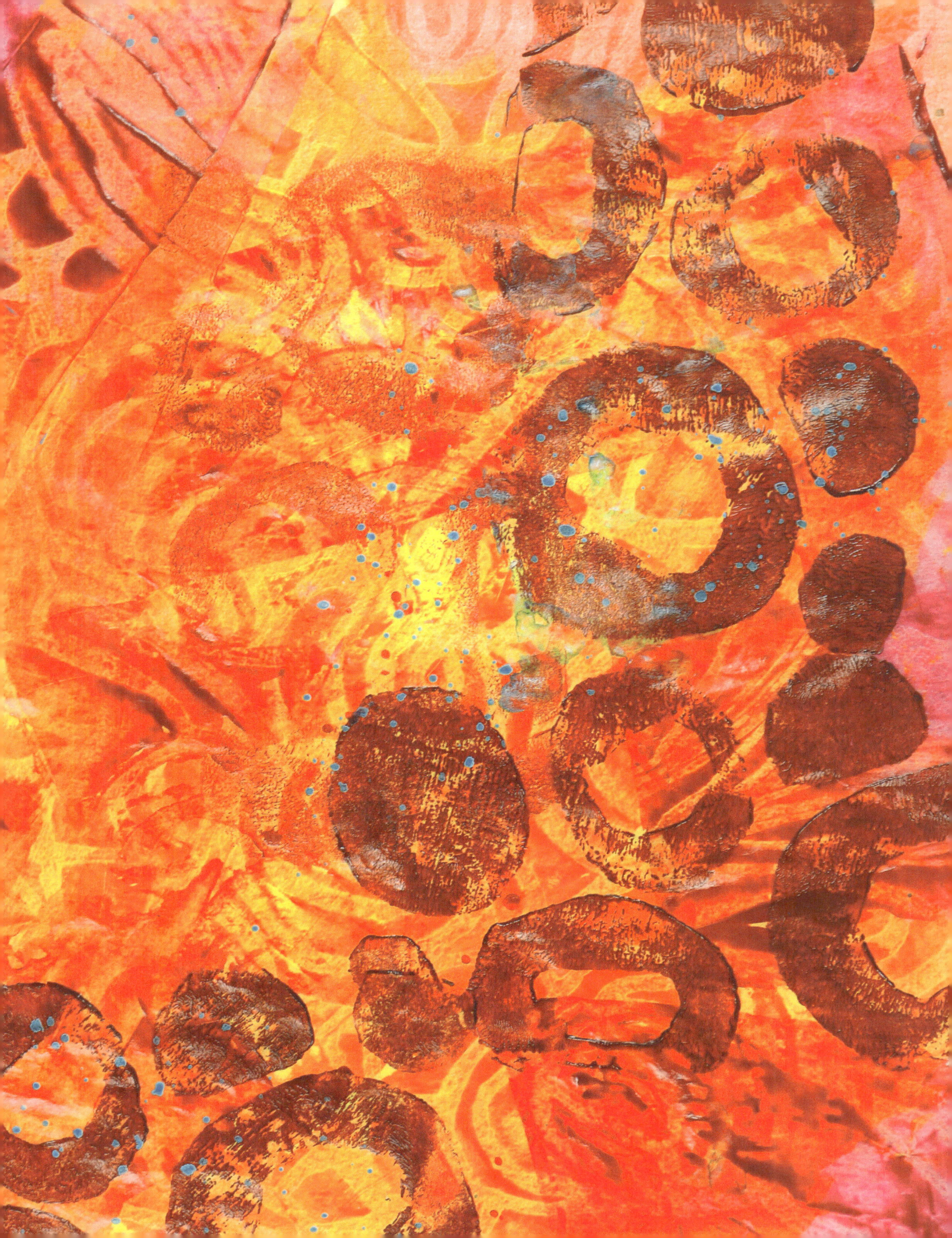

stamps

subtle subtraction

Hand-carved and commercially purchased stamps offer wonderful textures on the Gel Press printing plate. Pressing a stamp into the paint layer removes it subtly, revealing the pattern in a painterly impression. Overlapping and combining stamps with other effects offers more variety and interesting results.

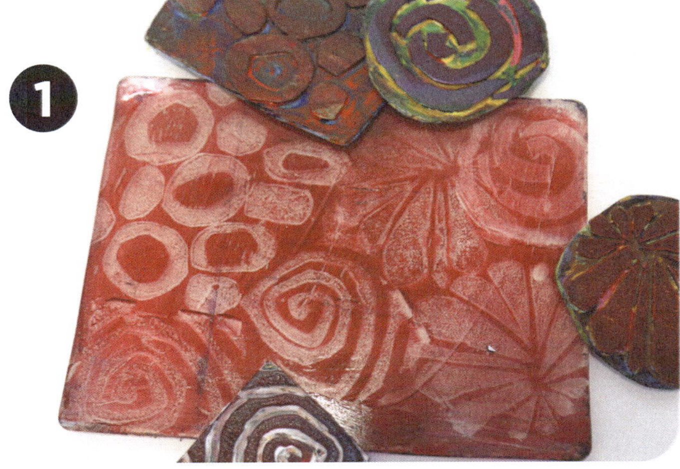

Removing paint with a clean, dry stamp pressed into it will create a subtle pattern on the plate.

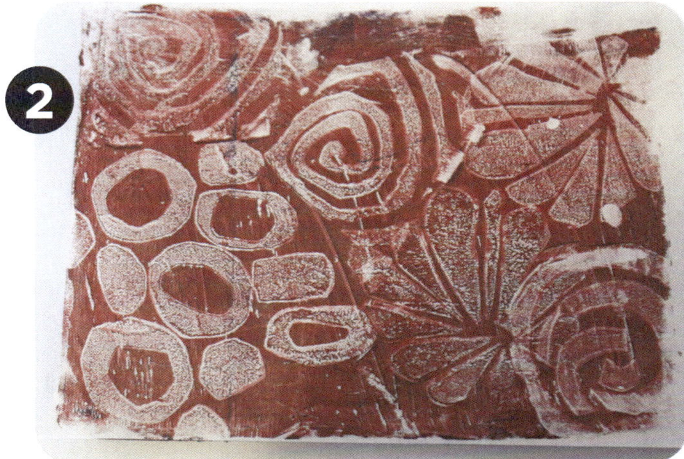

A print on white paper of the stamped plate.

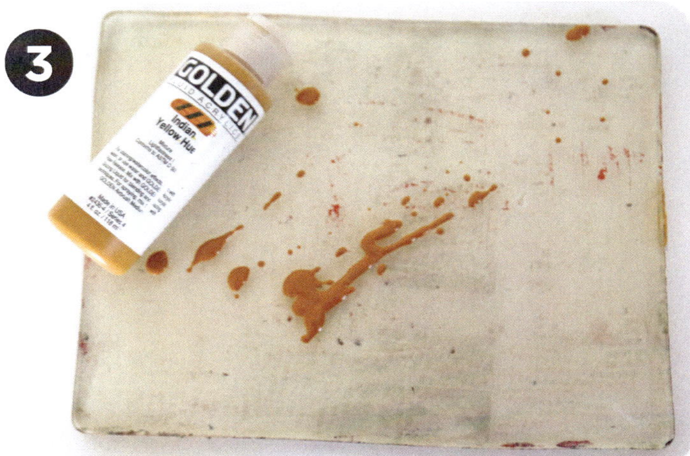

Set up the plate with a thin layer of light gold.

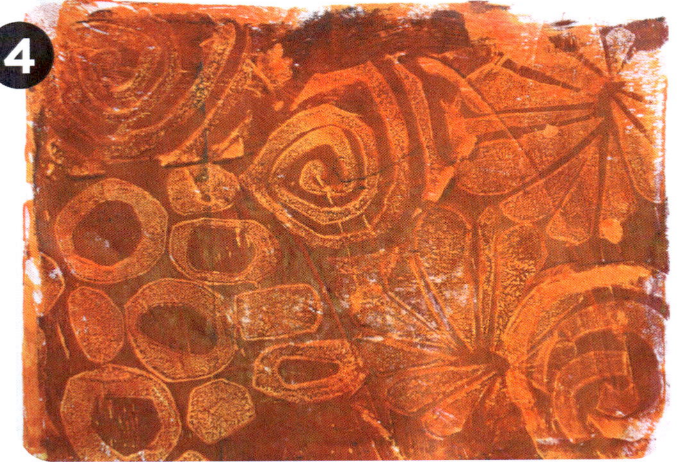

Overprint the light gold onto the pulled red print to tone down the whites.

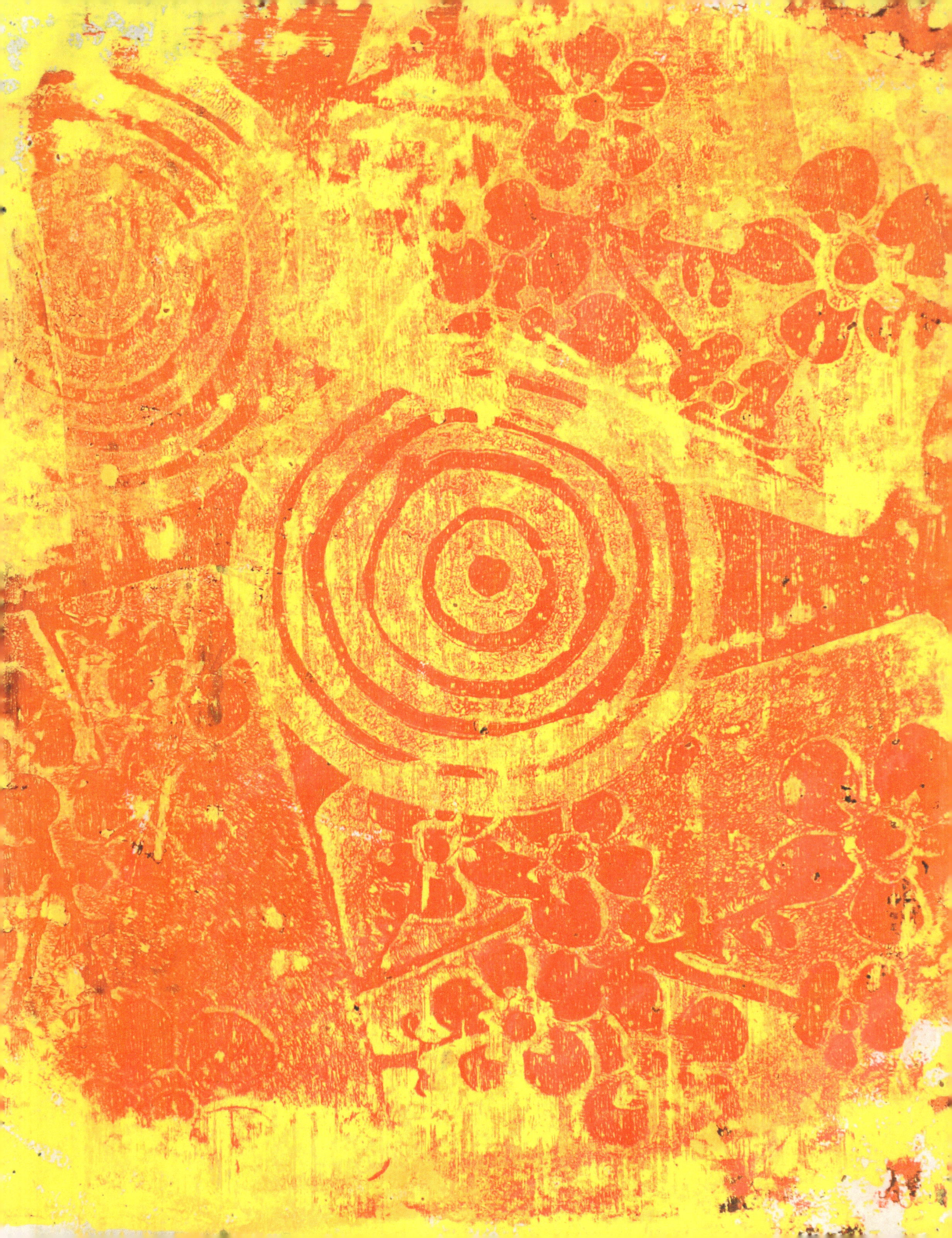

stamps

overlaying and multiplying

Hand-carved and commercially purchased stamps offer wonderful textures on the Gel Press printing plate. Pressing a stamp into the paint layer removes it subtly, revealing the pattern in a painterly impression. Overlapping and combining stamps with other effects offers more variety and interesting results.

Work over a previously pulled base layer.

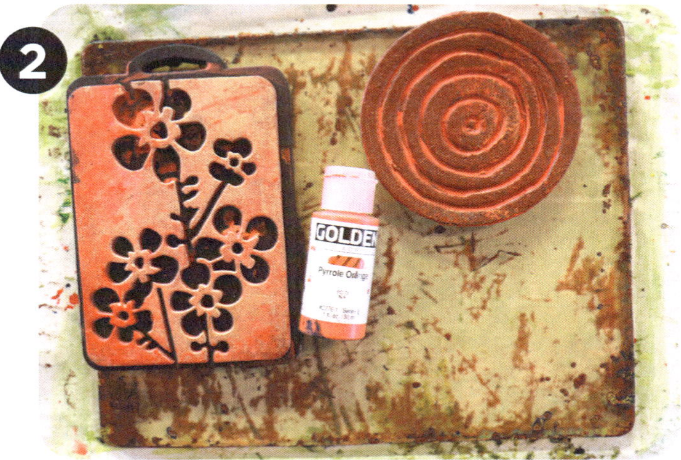

Utilizing multiple hand-carved and commercial stamps.

Press the clean, dry stamping tools into a thin layer of paint to remove it in a pattern, overlapping impressions for painterly effects.

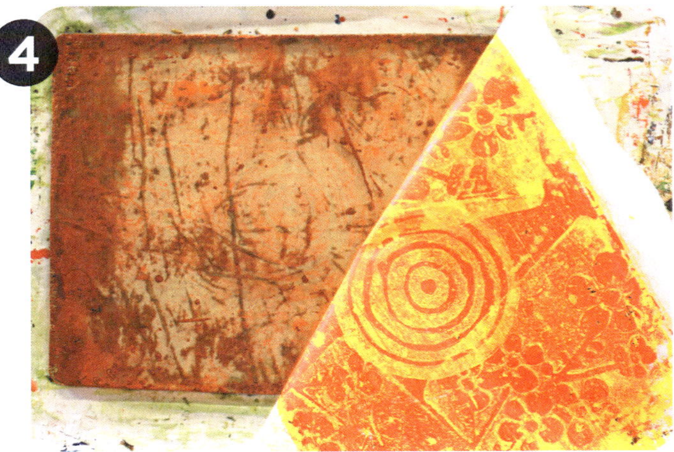

The yellow base layer shows through the areas in which the paint was removed by the overlapping stamps.

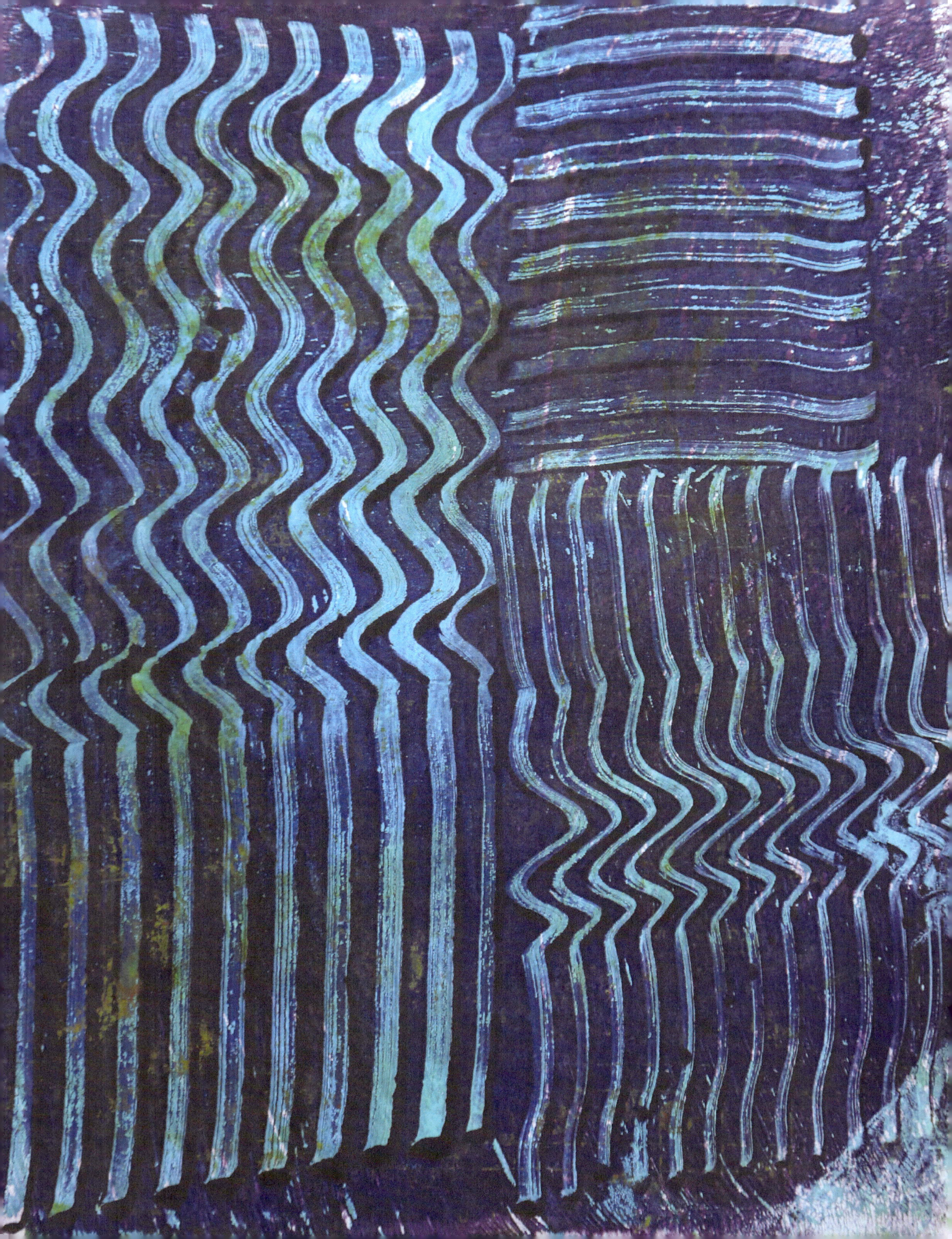

scrapers

catalyst wedges

Princeton makes a line of hand held wedge tools with teeth on two edges. They fit nicely in the palm of your hand and come in many different widths and patterns for scraping. The wedges work wonderfully on the Gel Press printing plate to scrape in straight, wiggle, zig zag or any combination of motions to create interesting patterns scraped out of (removing) the paint.

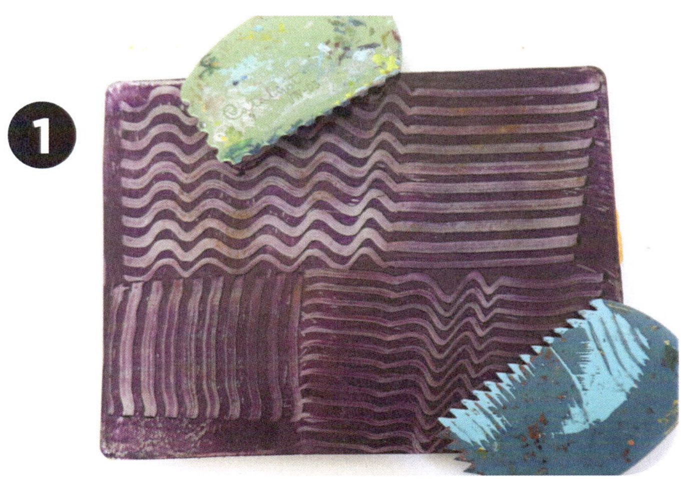

Remove paint from the plate with the scrapers.

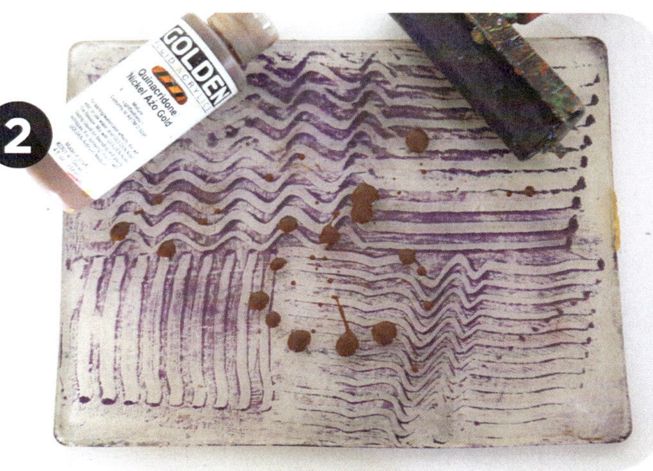

Apply a thin layer of light brown paint to the residual paint after pulling the first print.

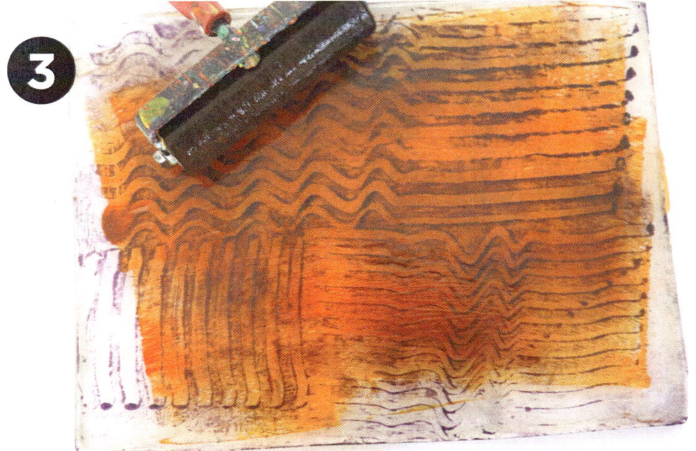

The brown paint and residual paint layer will pull off together for a subtle, painterly print.

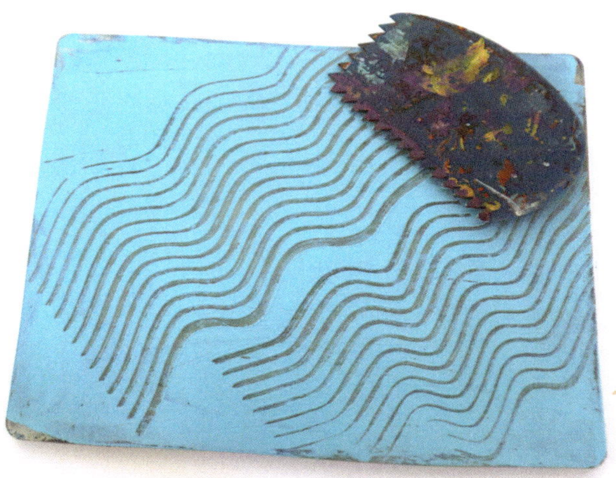

Remove paint from the plate with the scrapers.

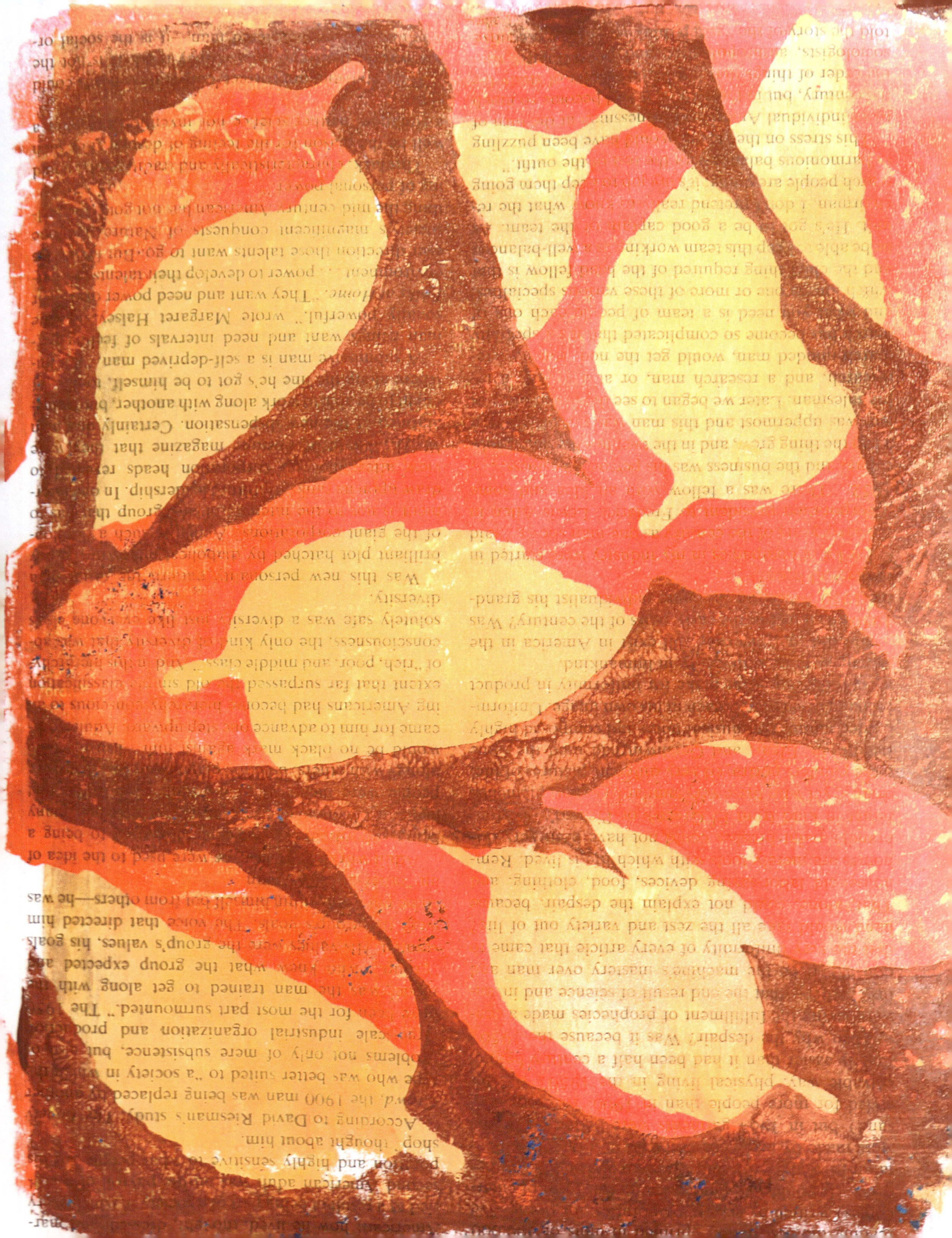

position and highly sensitive to
shop thought about him.

According to David Riesman's study of [...]
[...]rd, the 1900 man was being replaced by another
[...]e who was better suited to "a society in which the
[...]oblems not only of mere subsistence, but
[...]cale industrial organization and prod[...]
[...] for the most part surmounted." The
[...] the man trained to get along with [...]
[...] knew what the group expected a[...]
[...] values were the group's values, his goals
[...] The voice that directed him
[...] himself from others—he was

[...] but in [...]
for more people than [...]
[...]ay, physical living in the [...]
[...]an it had been half a century
[...] despair? Was it because [...]
[...] fulfillment of prophecies made a[...]
[...] the end result of science and in [...]
[...] machine's mastery over man a[...]
[...]rmity of every article that came
[...]ere all the zest and variety out of li[...]
[...] not explain the despair, becau[...]
[...] devices, food, clothing, a[...]
[...] took with which [...] is lived. Rem-

[...] in the Uniform-
[...]rmity in product
[...]ankind.
[...] in America in the
[...]s of the century? Was
[...]idualist his grand-

[...]es in my industry [...] started in
[...] Francis [...] Lutten call[...]
[...]re was a fellow [...]
[...] the business was [...]
[...] the thing grew, and in the [...]
[...] was uppermost and this man [...]
[...]lesman. Later we began to see [...]
[...], and a research man, or a[...]
[...]nded man, would get the no[...]
[...]ecome so complicated that [...] spe[...]
[...] need is a team of peo[...] each on[...]
[...] one or more of these various specia[...]
[...] the [...]thing required of the [...] fellow is [...]
[...] be able [...] p this team working [...] well-balanc[...]
[...] He's go[...] be a good cap[...] of the team [...]
[...]rman, I don[...] pretend rea[...] know what the re[...]
[...]ch people are [...] if [...] to keep them going
[...]armonious bal[...] the [...] the outfit."
[...]his stress on the [...] have been puzzling
[...]individual A[...] nessm[...] a[...]n of
[...]century, but [...]
[...]der of thin[...]
[...]ociologists, a[...] m[...]
[...] told the story [...]

[...]d be no black mark again[...] him
came for him to advance on[...] step upward. A[...]
ing Americans had become[...] hierarchy conscious to [...]
extent that far surpassed [...] old sim[...] classification
of "rich, poor, and middle class." And in this hi[...] pre[...]
consciousness, the only kind of diversity [...] was ab-
solutely safe was a diversi[...] just like ever[...]one e[...]
diversity.

Was this new personality [...] nature[...] [...] [...]
brilliant plot hatched by diabolic[...] [...] [...]
of the giant corporatior [...] [...] such a [...]
[...] group that [...]
[...] h[...] dership. In e[...]
[...]on heads re[...] to
[...] magazine that [...]
[...]ensation. Certainly [...]
[...] work along with another, b[...]
[...] ne he's got to be himself, t[...]
[...] e man is a self-deprived man [...]
[...] want and need intervals of fe[...]
[...]owerful." wrote Margaret Halsey [...]
Home. "They want and need power [...]
[...]ent . . . power to develop their talents [...]
[...]ection those talents want to go. But [...]
[...]s magnificent conquests of Nature [...]
[...] the mid-century American has not go[...]
[...]sonal mov[...]
[...] characteristically and tradi[...]
[...] the coming of do[...]
[...]iselle [...] inv[...]
[...]ot the
[...] in the social or-

leaves

positive and negative

Freshly picked leaves make lovely masks and positive prints. In Florida we have some HUGE leaves, but a combination of small and medium leaves work just as nicely. Experiment with different types, ferns always offer very interesting shapes.

A base layer of light yellow over found paper.

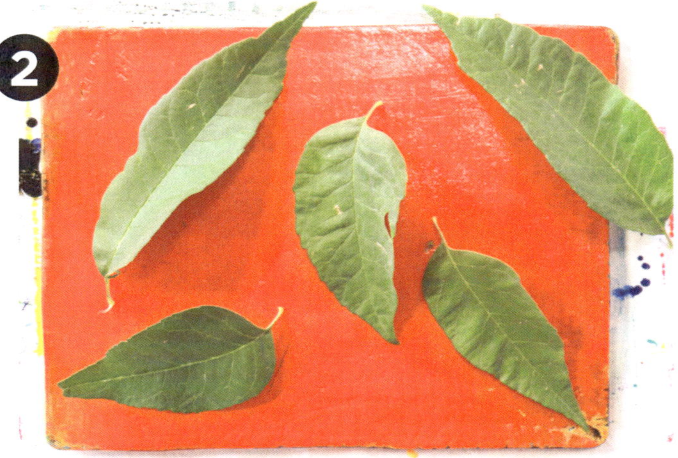

Lay the leaves vein side down into the paint

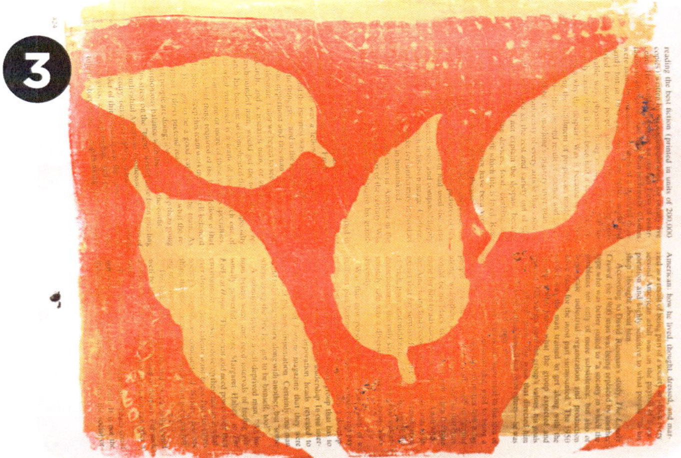

The first leaf layer in orange working over the pre-printed light yellow base layer.

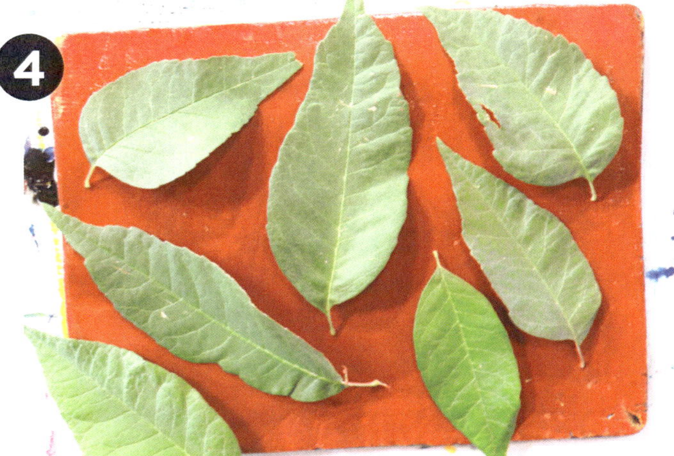

Change the position of the leaves on a slightly darker paint and reprint over the first leaf layer (left).

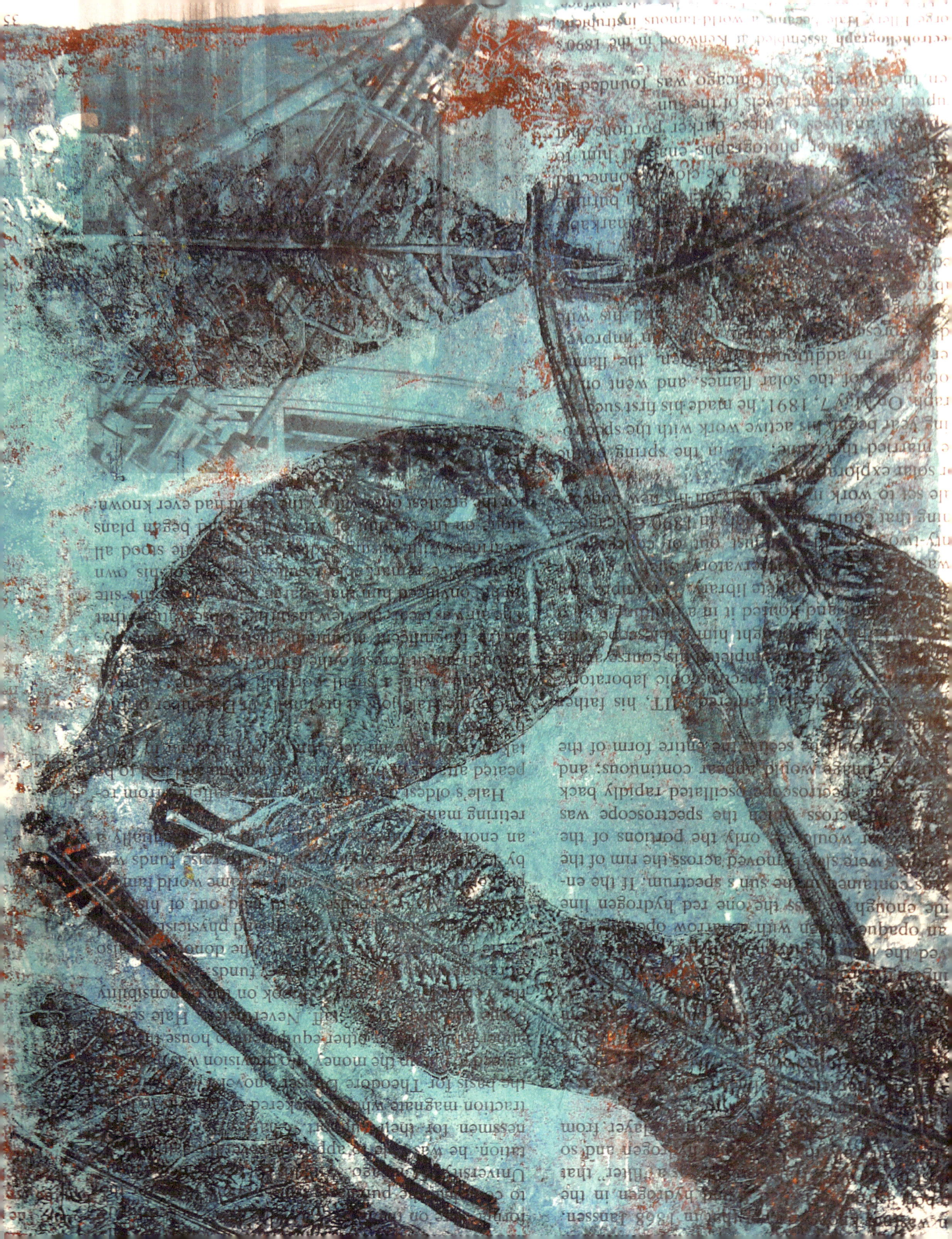

hydrogen, in the ... a filter" that ... hydrogen and so ... layer from ...

an opaque ... with a narrow opening ... ide enough to pass the one red hydrogen line ... was contained in the sun's spectrum. If the en... ...were slowly moved across the rim of the ...ar would... only the portions of the ...across, which the spectroscope was ...spectroscope oscillated rapidly back ...image would appear continuous; and ...would... seeing the entire form of the

...had entered MIT, his father ...scopic laboratory ...completed his cons... ...aught him a telescope with ...and housed it in a ...plete library. It is simple ...observatory... ...ty-two... just out of colleg... ...ing that could... in 1890 Chicago— ...le set to work ... on his new one ...r solar explorat... ...married that June; ... in the spring of the ...ng year began his active work with the sp... ...raph On May 7, 1891, he made his first succ... ...ot... of the solar flames, and went on ... ...in addition... ...en, the flam... ...ress... ...d he will... ...abr... ...ed... ...markab... ...th burning ...clowly connected ... ...photographs enabled him to ...cal analyses of these darker portions that ...upted from deeper levels of the sun. ...en the University of Chicago was founded...

...to ... the pun... University of Chicago ...tation. he was ... app... ...nessmen for the ... ...traction magnate who ...kered ... ...the basis for Theodore D... ...novel ...in the money ... provision w... ...other equip... to house th... ...staff. Nevertheless Hale set ... ...ook on ... responsibility ...funds. ...the donor ... also ...physicist ...ould out of his ...ame world fam... ...by ... ...size funds w... ...an enor... ...tially a ...retiring man...

Hale's oldest ... suffered from re-peated att... ...mountain had to be tak... ... Pasadena in ... ...Hale took a brief ... December of ... ...when a small-portable telescope ...ught ... at forge of the 6000 fo... ...magnificent mountain distant... ...air was clear the view insur... that ...onvinced him that ... ...site ...give remark... ...his own ...marines... ...stood all ...alone on the top of Mt W... ...began plans ...the greatest observatory the world had ever known.

...electroheliograph assembled at Kenwood in the 1890's ...orge Ellery Hale became a world-famous instrument ...

leaves

positive and negative

Freshly picked leaves make lovely masks and positive prints. In Florida we have some HUGE leaves, but a combination of small and medium leaves work just as nicely. Experiment with different types, ferns always offer very interesting shapes.

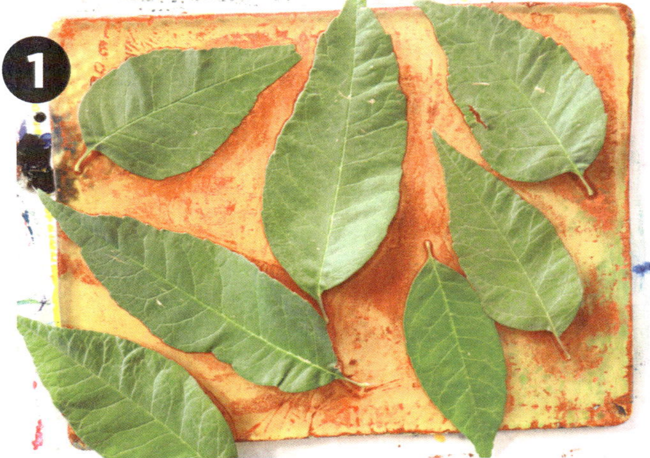

The leaves have trapped paint underneath after the first print is pulled.

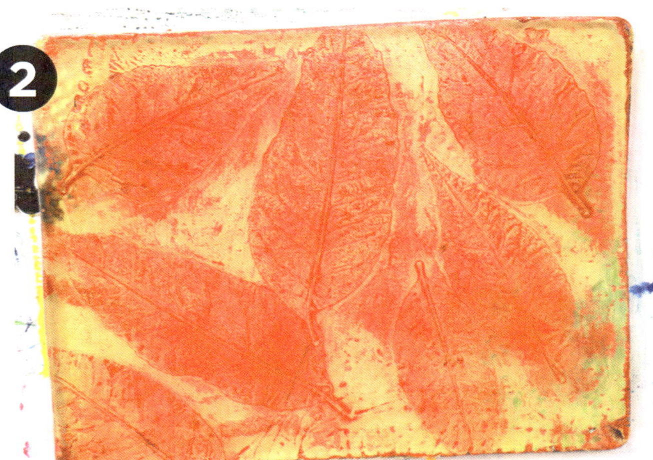

Gently removed the leaves to reveal the *ghost print* with excellent vein patterns.

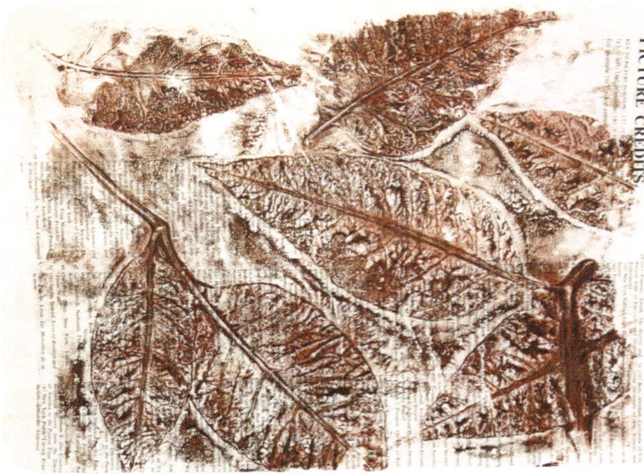

Example of a positive leaf print with trapped paint

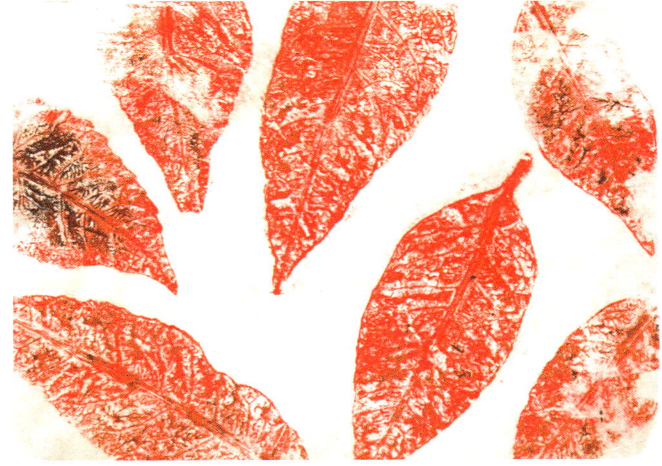

Example of a positive leaf print with trapped paint

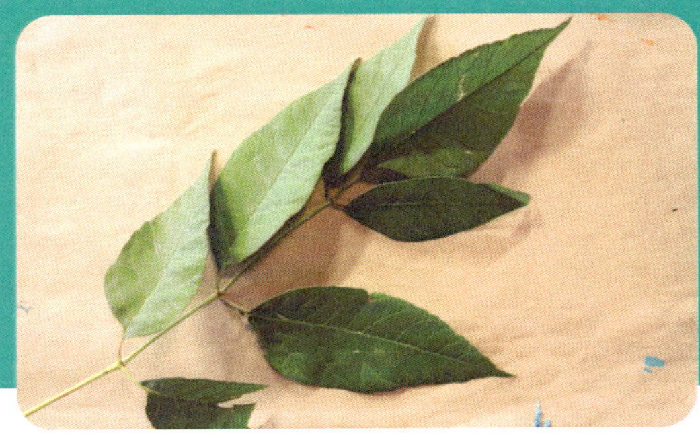

TIP

Fresh leaves work much better than dry ones. If you want to keep leaves fresh in the studio, put them into a gallon sized zip lock bag with a couple of wet paper towels. This will keep them softer for longer periods of time.

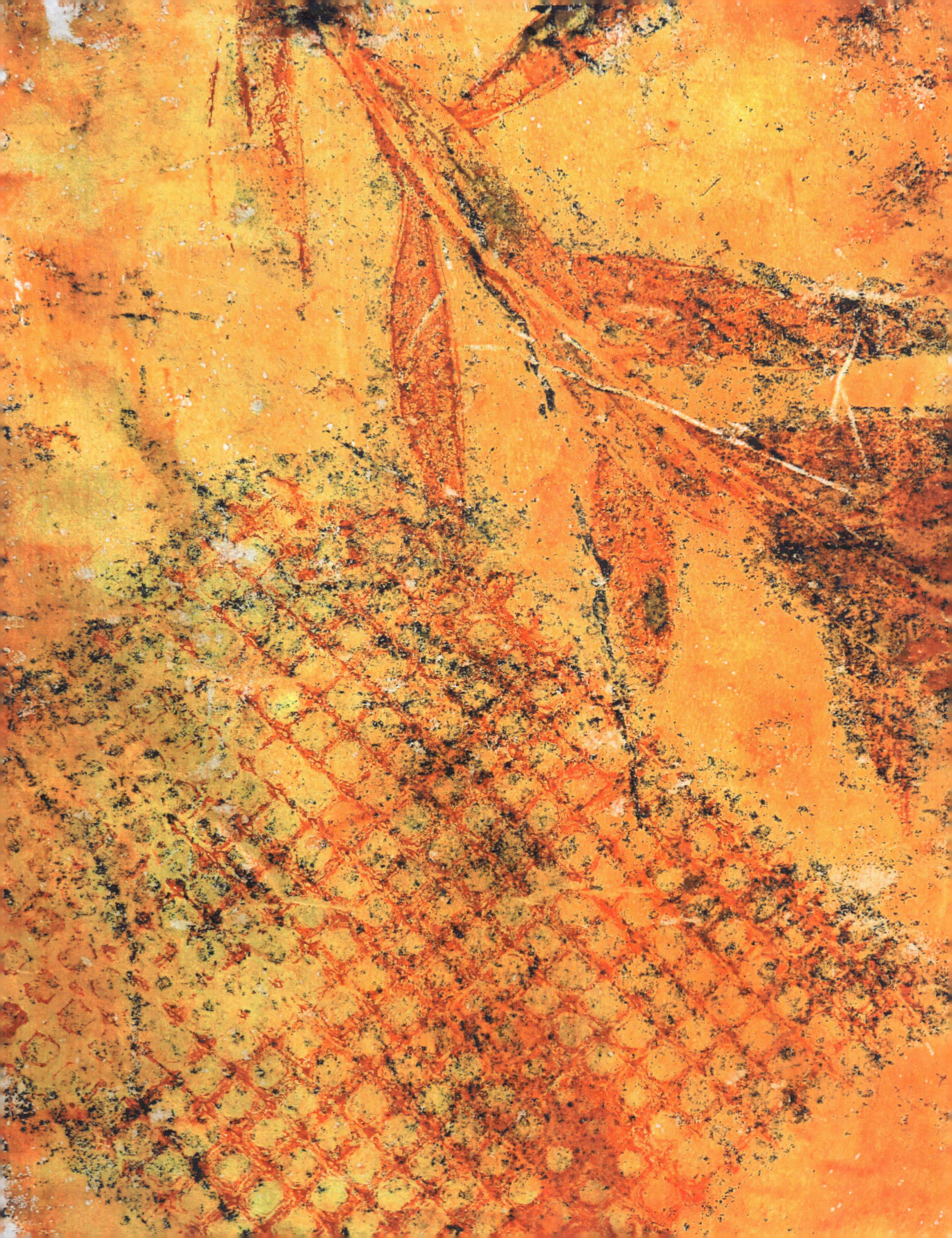

non slip
carpet pads

Non slip carpet pads are made from a squishy material that works well as a mask on the Gel Press printing plate. You can apply pressure with the heel of your hand in order to really get the paper to work its way down through the holes in the carpet pad. Occasionally lift up the corner of your page to be sure you are getting good contact, if not, lay the sheet back down and apply more pressure.

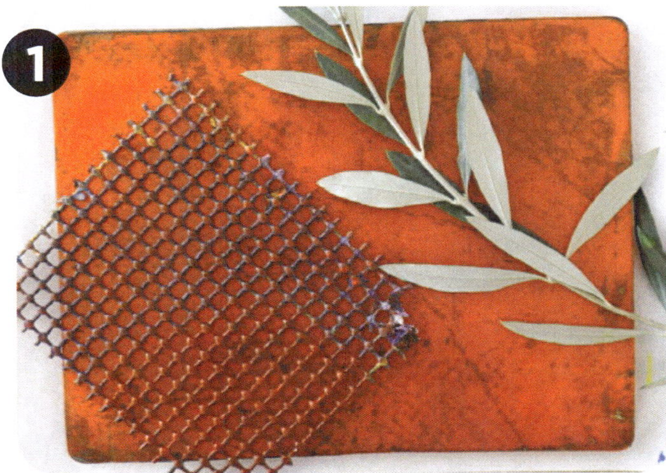

Carpet pad combined with an olive branch.

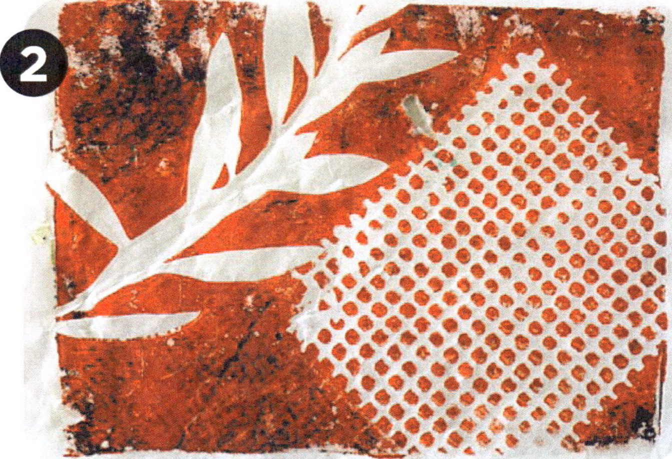

The carpet pad and olive branch mask the paint from the paper, the print picks up residual paint.

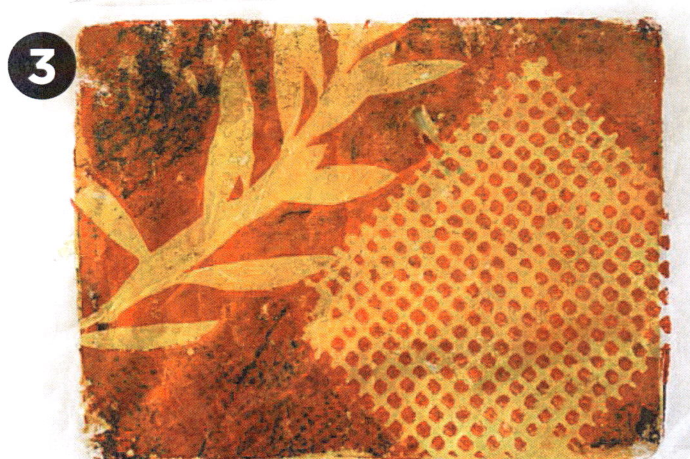

Lay a solid print of yellow *on top* of the original carpet pad print (left).

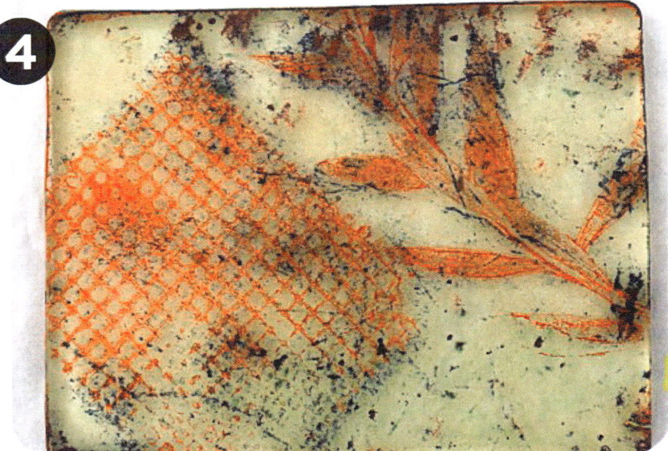

Trapped paint underneath the carpet pad and leaves, pull a *ghost* print onto a new sheet of paper with a light colored base layer.

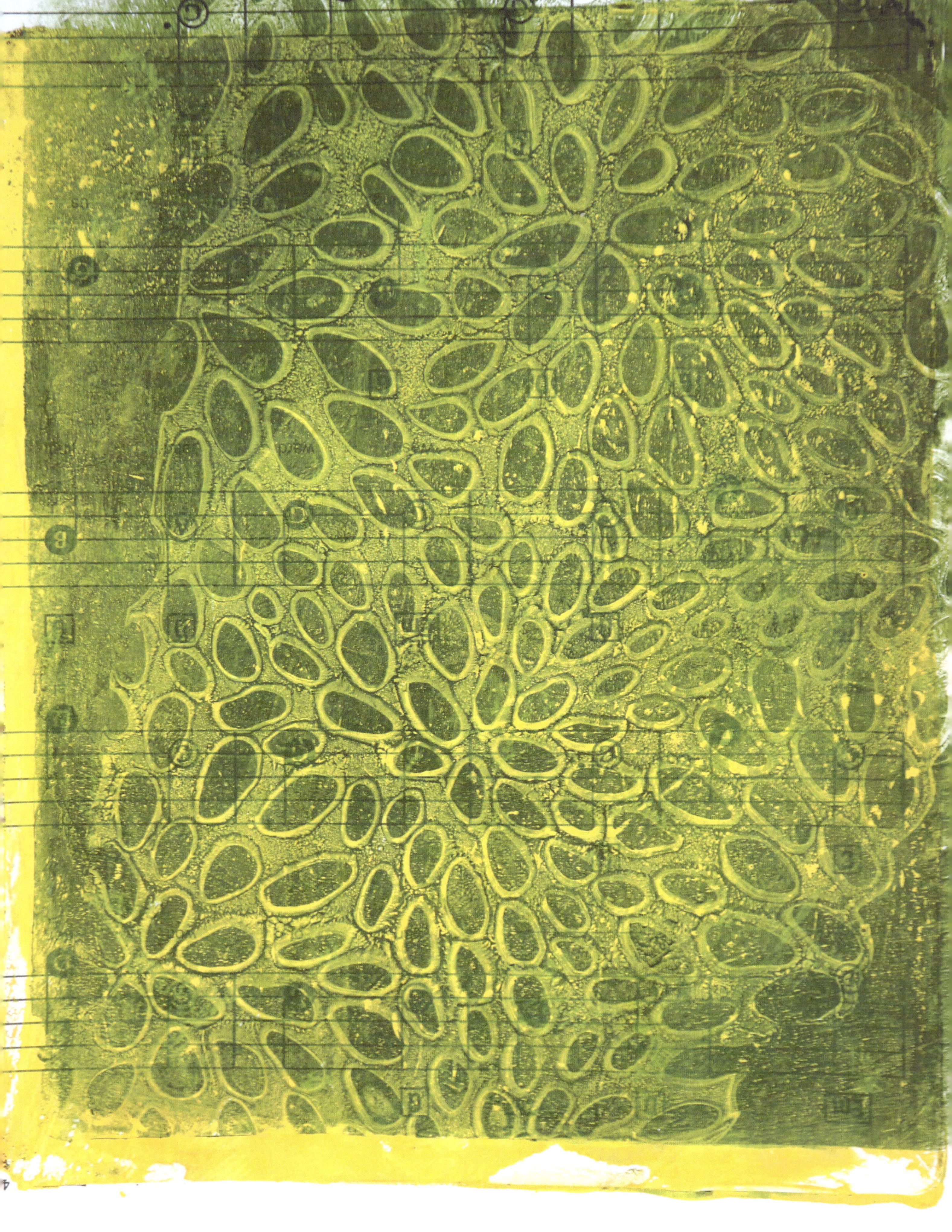

kitchen items

silicone sink liners and place mats

Silicone sink liners make wonderful Gel Press printing plate tools as do their cousins, silicone place mats. The sink liners I found on an end cap at Lowe's Home Improvement, then I found more patterns of them on *Amazon.com* and at Marshall's. The place mats honestly were a gift from a former student (*thank you Patty!*) who found them at Old Time Pottery in Orlando. She purchased an extra set for me, knowing I'd love and appreciate them. I cut the place mats in half, one for the studio and one for the classroom.

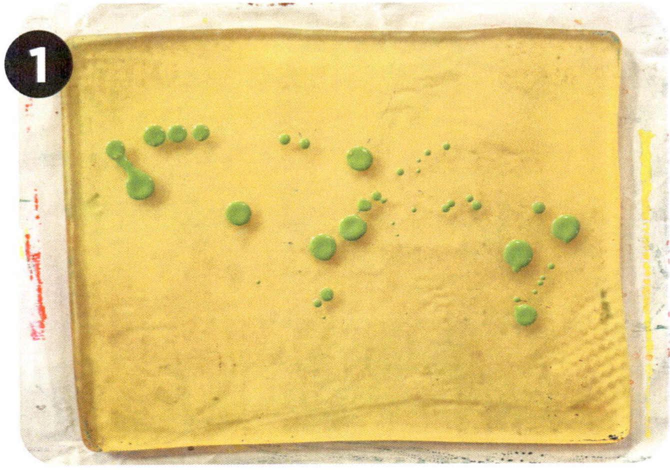

Spread a thin layer of light green on the plate.

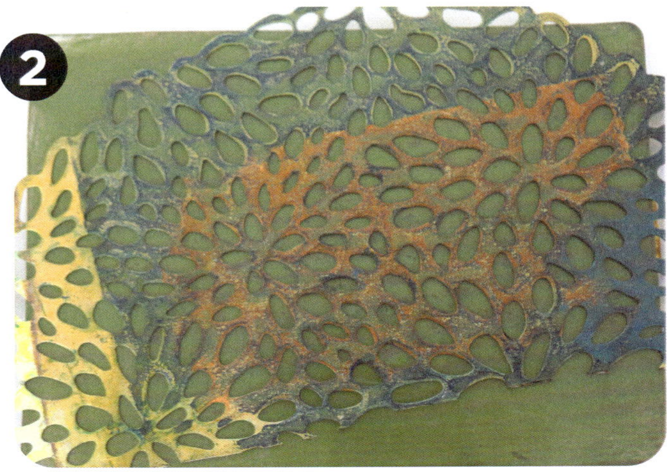

Press the clean, dry sink liner to remove paint.

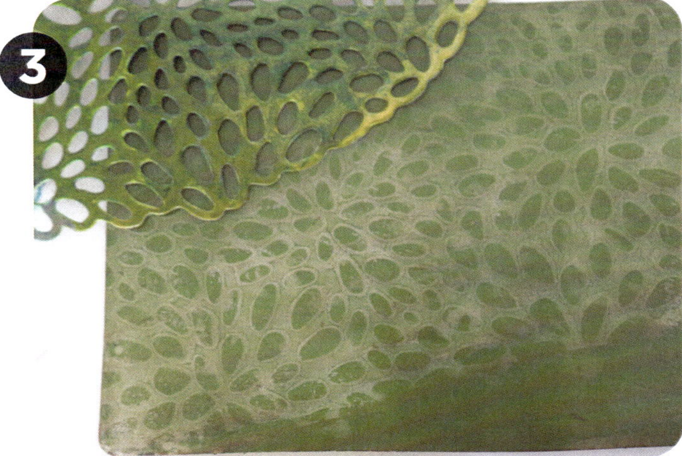

Lift the sink liner, removing paint to reveal a subtle pattern, print over the light yellow base layer.

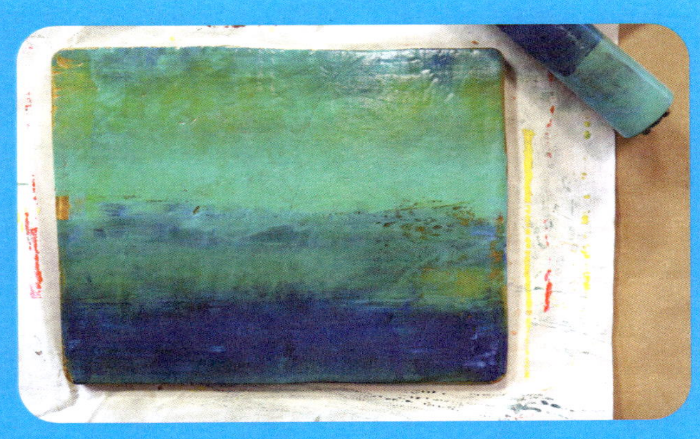

TIP

When applying paint to the Gel Press printing plate, you do not have to apply in only one color or even fully blended, experiment with mutlple colors in stripes or fields across the plate either in your light colored solid paper prep or in your layering techniques.

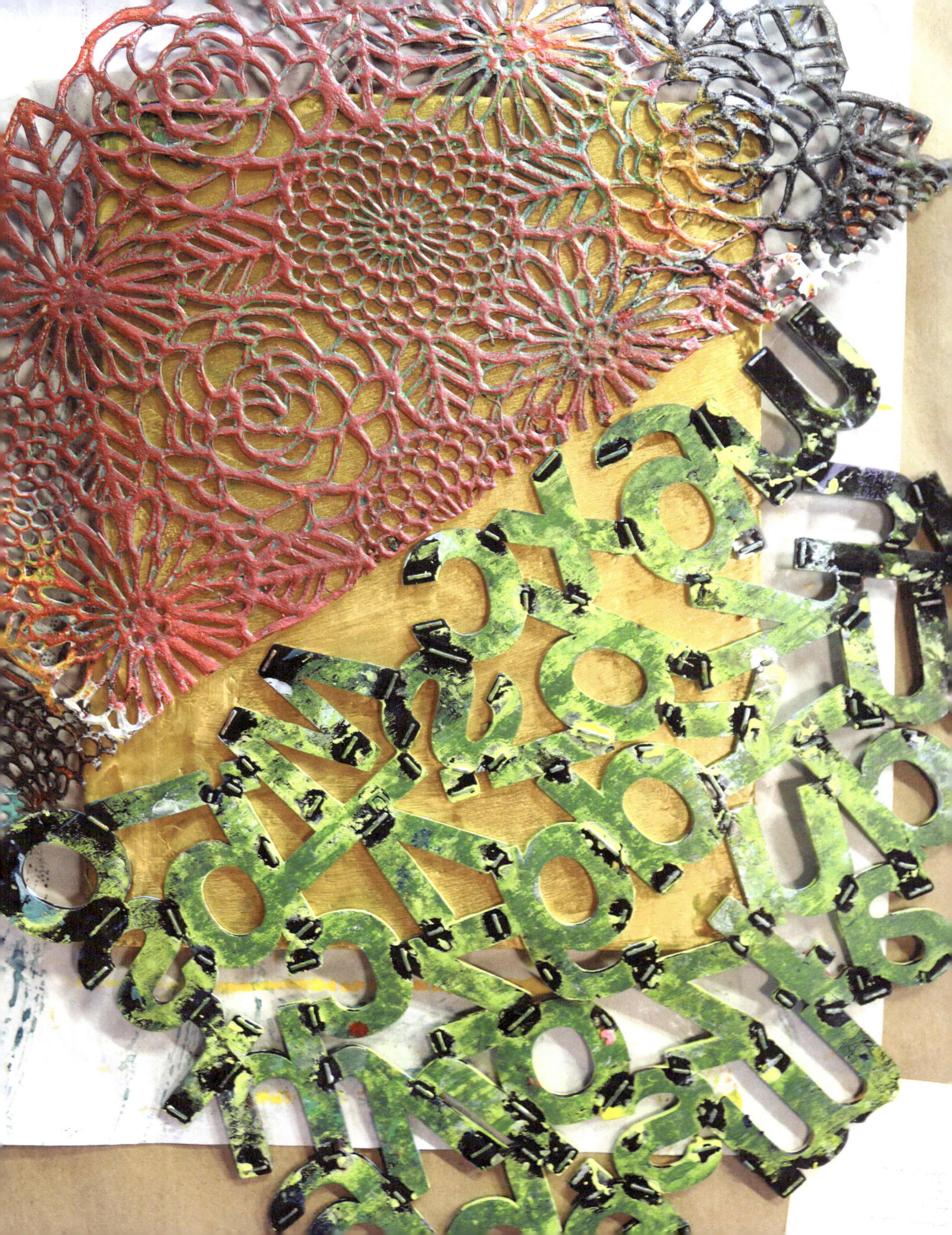

kitchen items

silicone place mats

Silicone sink liners make wonderful Gel Press printing plate tools as do their cousins, silicone place mats. My silicone place mats were a gift from a former student (*thank you Patty!*) who found them, envisioning their potential, at Old Time Pottery in Orlando. I cut the place mats in half, one for the studio and one for the classroom.

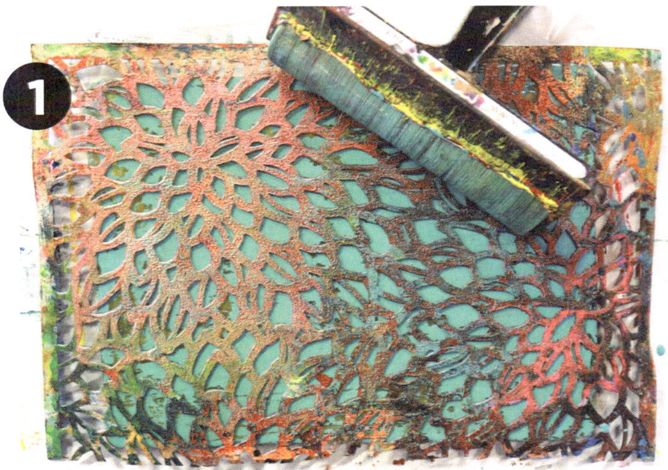

Use a brayer to apply pressure to the place mat.

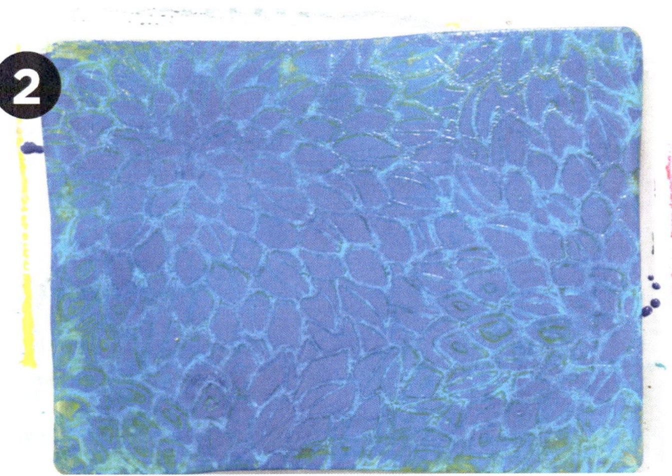

Paint removed in a subtle pattern.

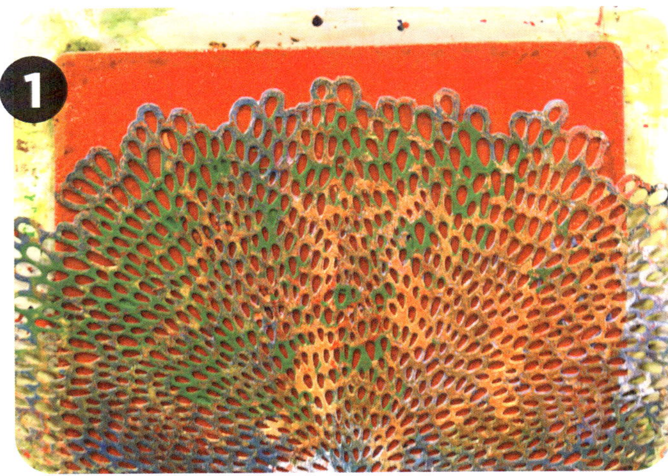

Press and lift the place mat, removing paint
in an organic pattern.

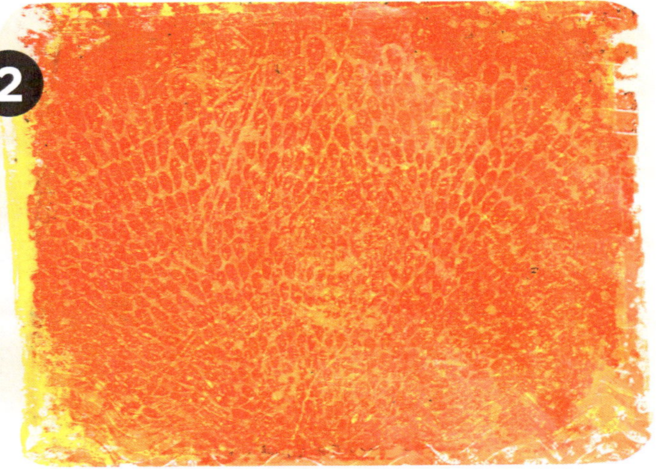

Print the red over a previously pulled
yellow base layer.

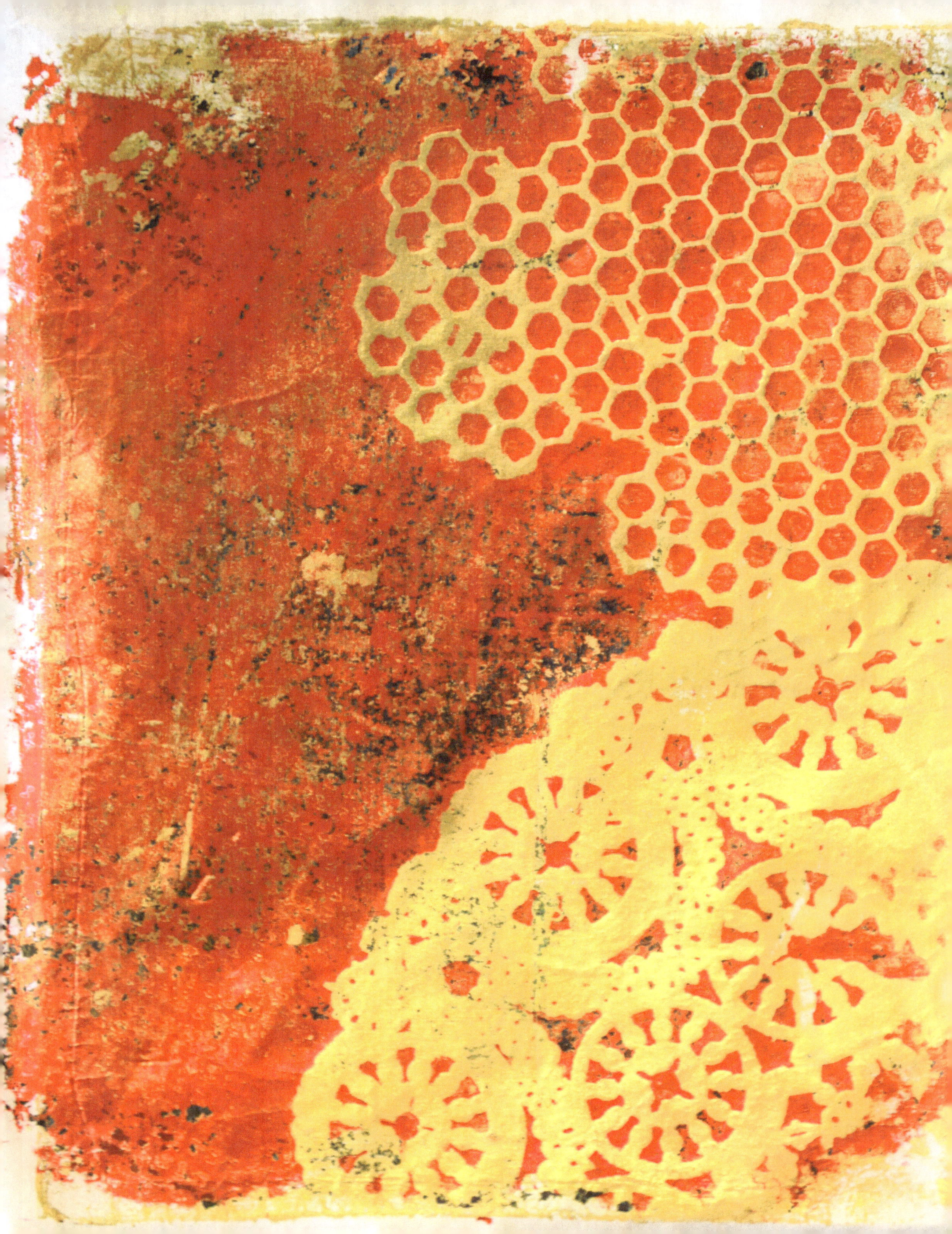

paper products

paper doilies

Paper doilies come in all shapes and sizes, from the ones you can purchase at the grocery store, to the ones you find in restaurant supply, to the Sunday brunch buffet of your breakfast joint. I have asked restaurant servers for doilies and they have gladly supplied me with a few of each size. Almost everyone wants to help an artist in her quest for creativity! Coat the doily both sides with gesso primer to seal and protect it from moisture, this will extend its' creative lifespan.

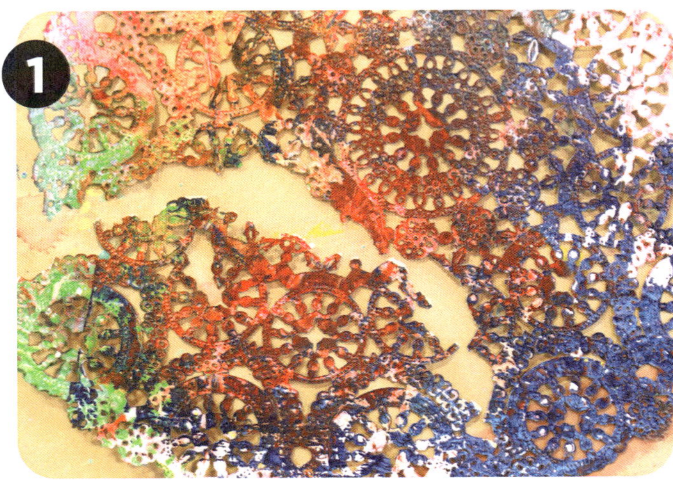

Commercial doilies come in larger sizes.

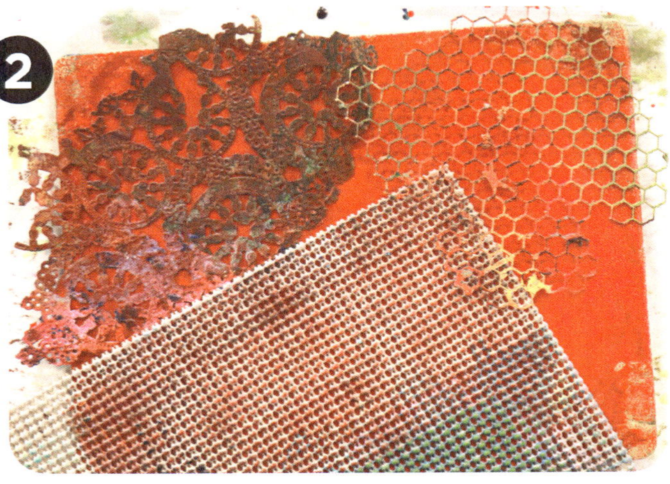

Combine a paper doily with a stencil and shelf liner, for an interesting combination.

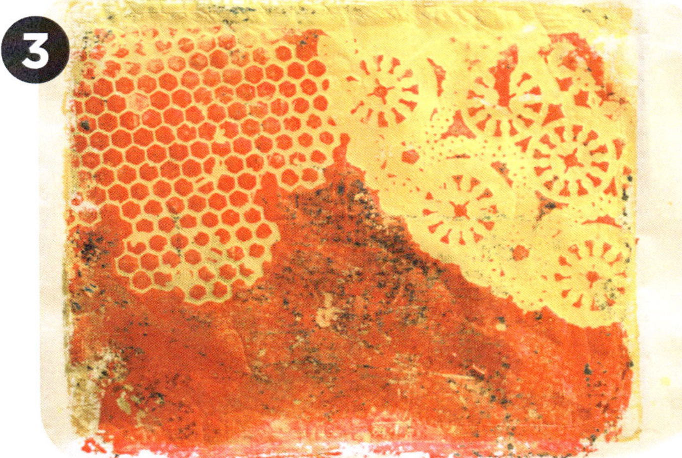

Print the red over the base layer gold, using the doily, the stencil and the shelf liner as masks (left).

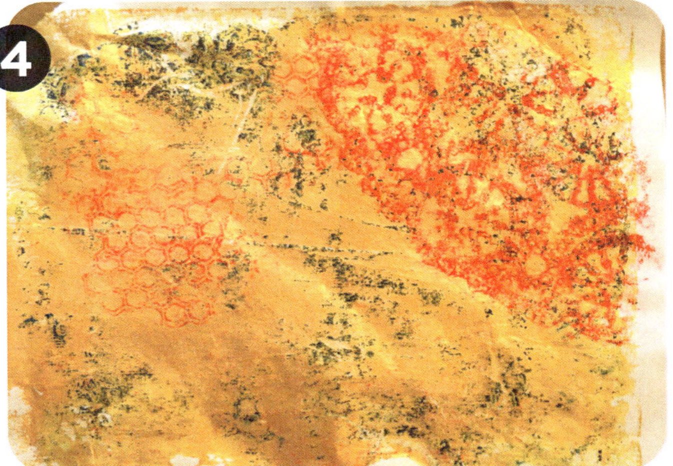

Pull the *ghost* print (paint remaining on the plate that was trapped under the masks) over a second gold base print with residual paint.

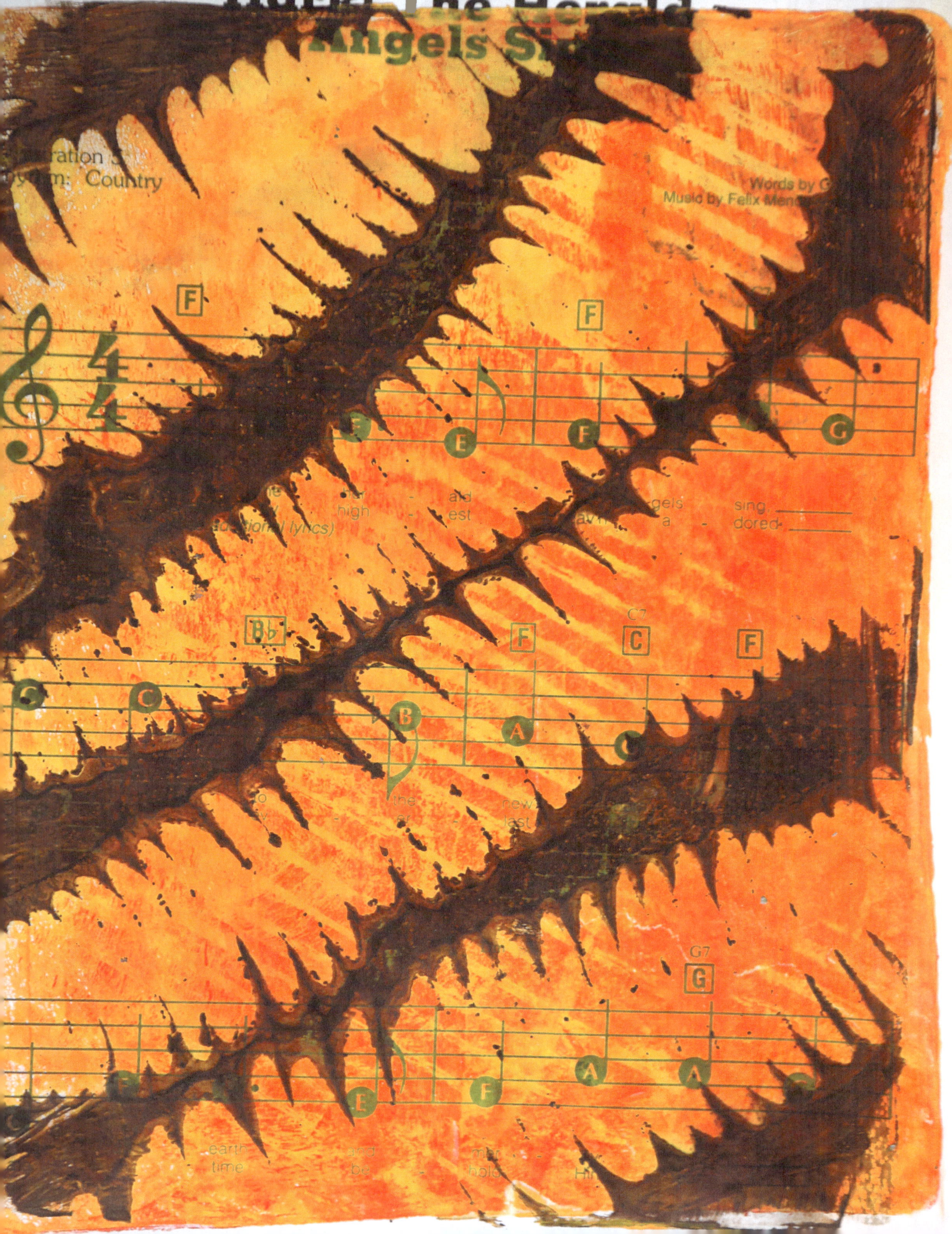
Hark! The Herald
Angels Sing
Words by G
Music by Felix Men
ration
ythm: Country
(additional lyrics)

paper products

corrugated cardboard

If you are an *Amazon.com* shopper like I am, this stuff just keeps arriving at your doorstep, for free! Simply peel off the top layer of paper to reveal the corrugation in the middle of the cardboard. A variety of widths can be found inside the walls of different corrugated boxes. As with paper doilies, always coat both sides of the cardboard with gesso primer to extend its' creative lifespan.

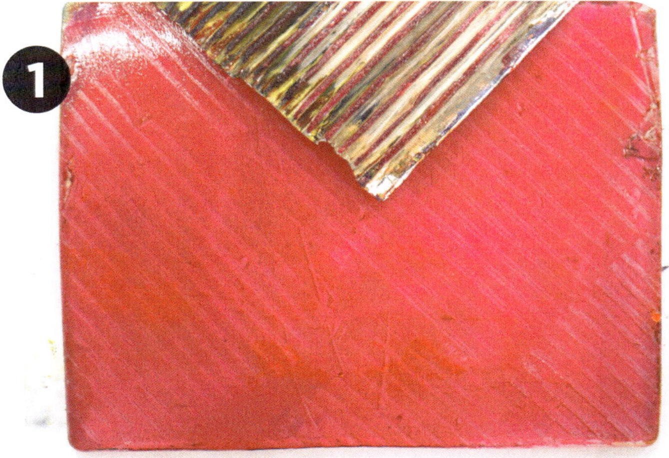

Press the cardboard into wet paint on the plate, removing paint to create an impression of the pattern.

Pull the first print and there will be a residual layer of corrugated pattern remaining on the plate.

Add a light layer of paint over the top of the dry residual corrugated pattern.

Pull a print of the magenta residual paint and the yellow overlay, together on found paper.

Left: A fresh ferns mask with dark blue/brown layered over the corrugated print from above.

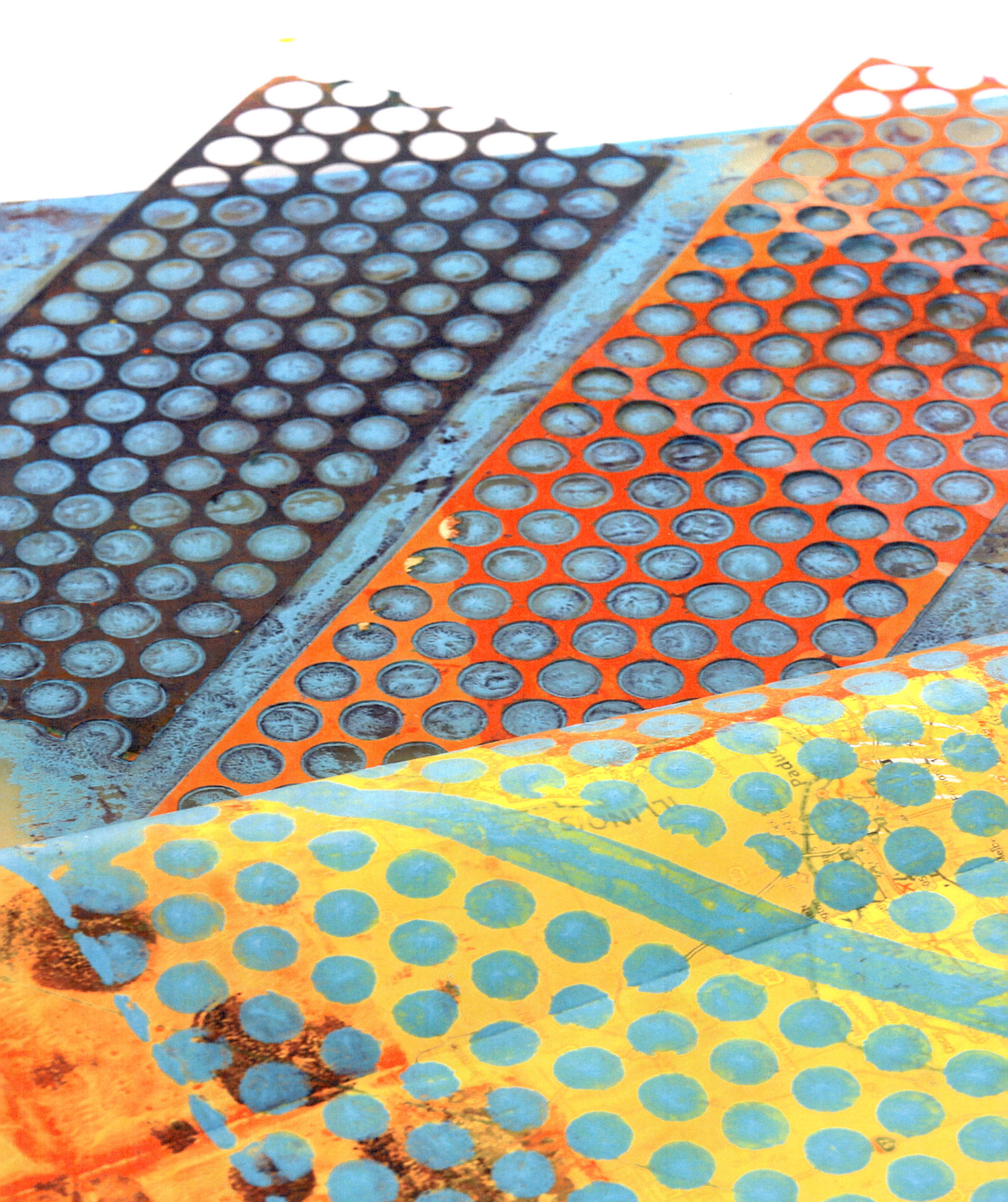

found objects

string, sequin waste, fiber sheet

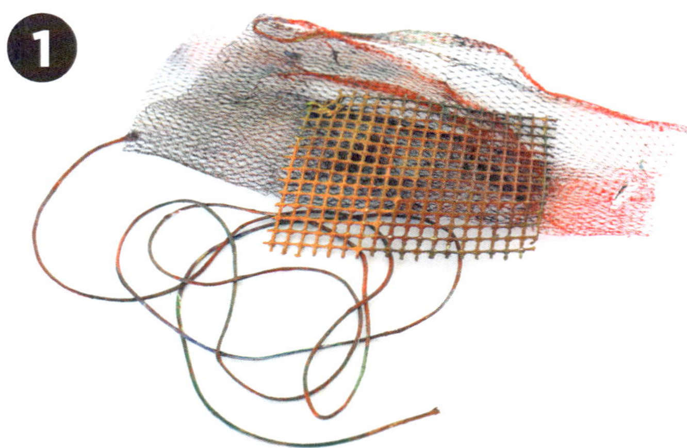

Metallic gift string, onion bag, carped pad.

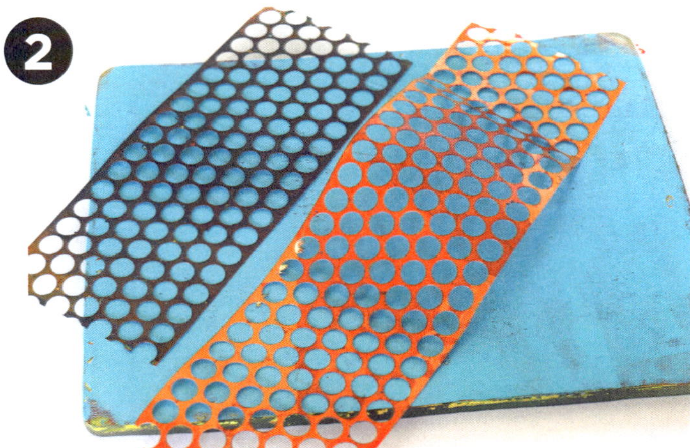

Sequin waste or *punchinella* from the craft store.

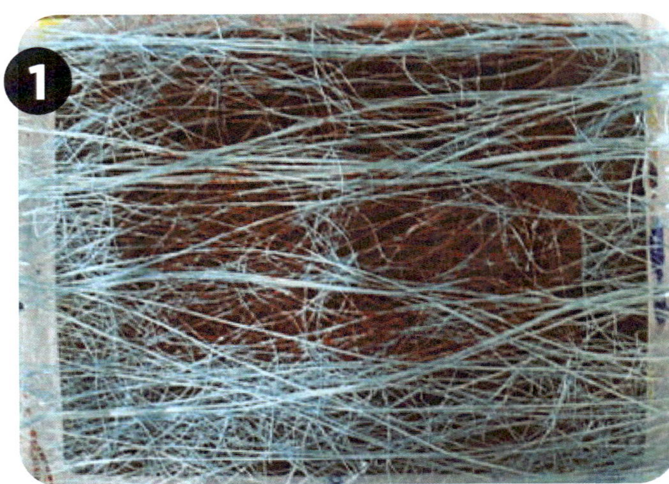

Fiber material over deep red paint on the plate,
used as a mask.

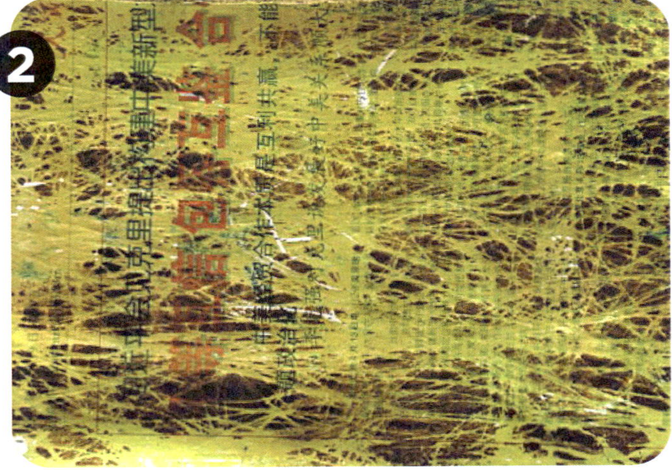

Deep red printed over light green, press with heels of
your hands for good, solid contact.

Left: Punchinella printed in an opaque teal paint over a light colored previous print (on a map)--multiplying layers.

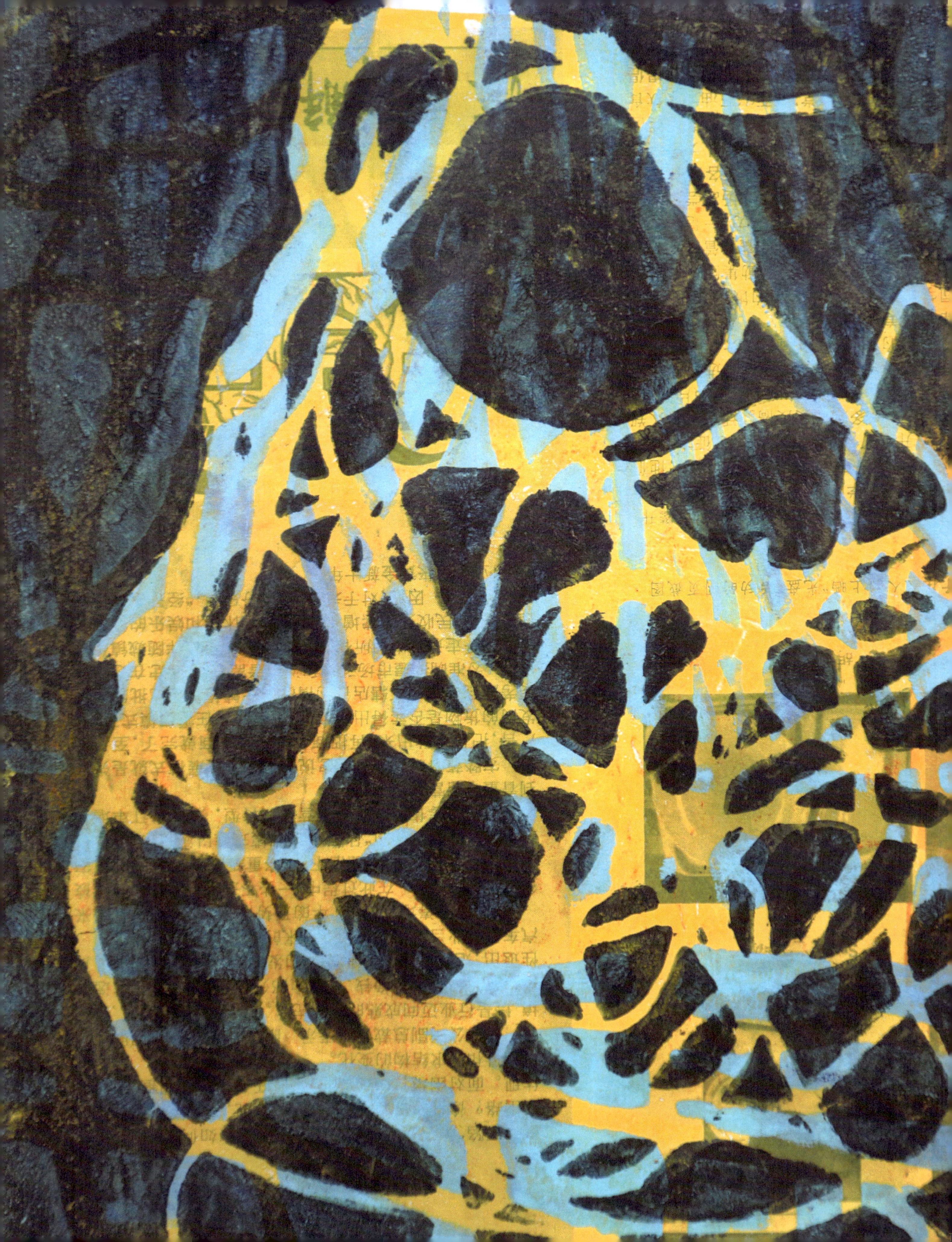

found objects

jute string and layering

A look around your home might reveal some wonderful objects for patterning on the Gel Press Plate. Here I am playing with jute string and taking advantage of additng it on top of some previous printed, lighter layers as well as using the ghost print from it to add on top of another ight colored solid layer. Sometimes the most creative art materials are found outside the art supply store.

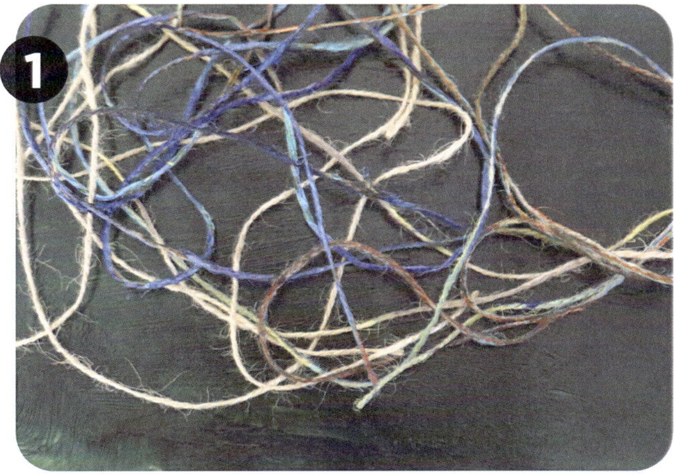

Jute string has a sligthly fuzzy edge, it's thin enough to yield detailed line patterns.

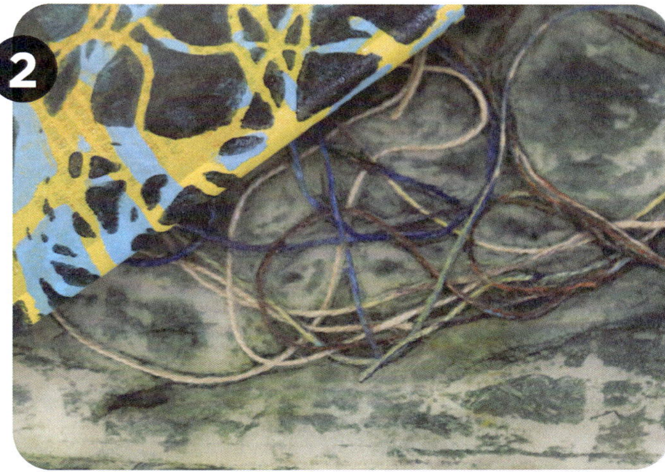

Pulling a print of the string on top of a prepared sheet.

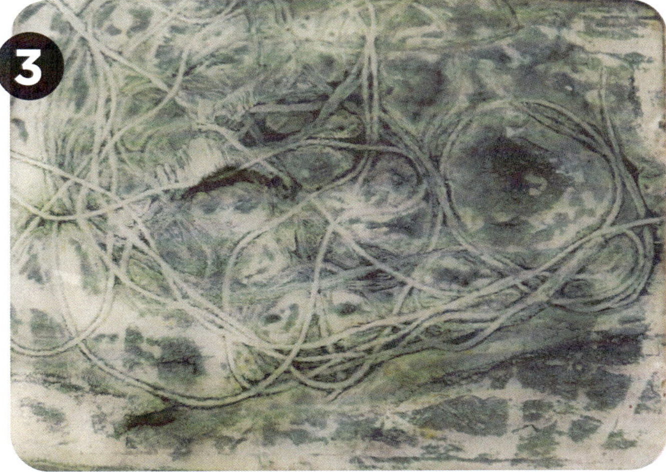

The ghost print after the first print is pulled, and the string is removed from the plate.

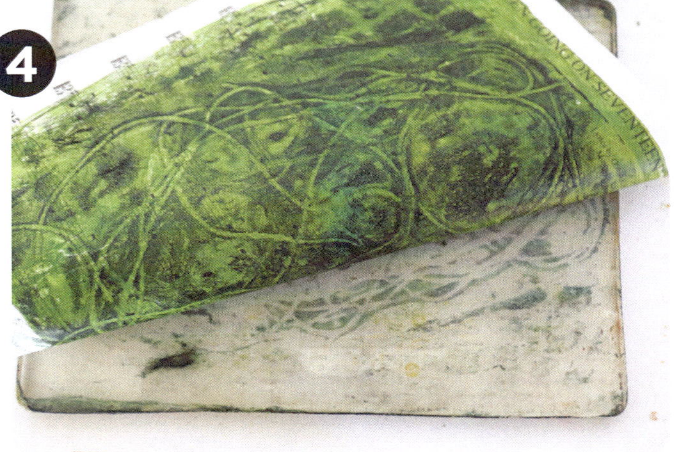

The ghost print applied over a light colored solid that was ready and waiting in the wings.

Left: String with dark green paint added over the top of a prepared sheet of yellow solid with teal stencil

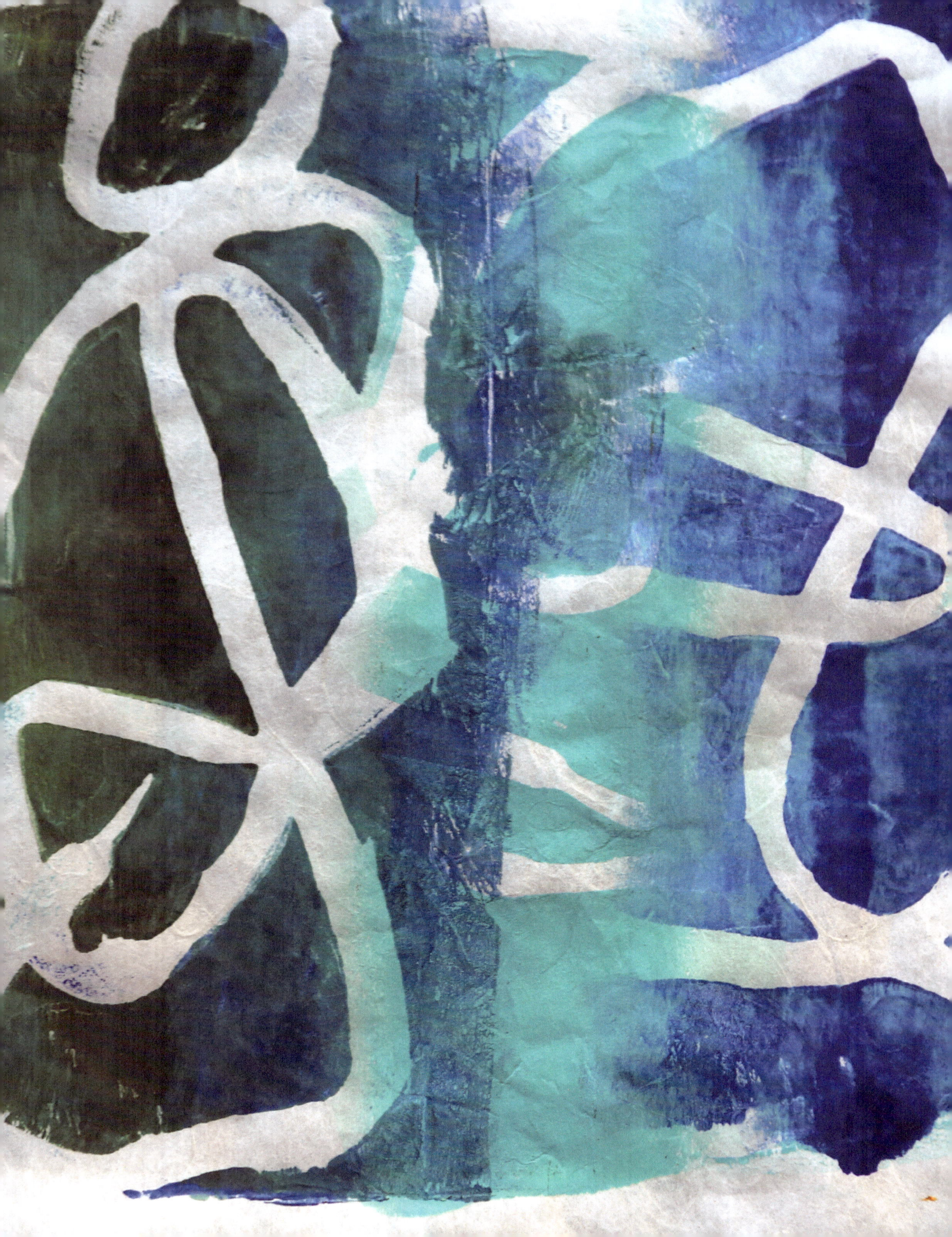

found objects

shoelaces and multiple colors

A look around your garage, recycle bin or trash might reveal some wonderful objects for patterning on the Gel Press Plate; after all, one man's junk is another man's treasure. These shoe laces were an alternate pair that came with my son's Nike sneakers. He threw them away, but I rescued them from the bin; hoarding in the name of art. These flat shoe laces are thicker than string or yarn and yield a totally different effect.

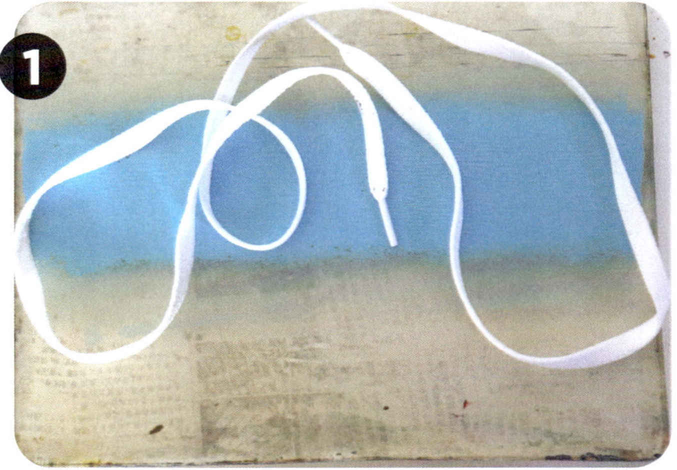

Spread the paint in a thin line on the plate, versus covering the entire surface.

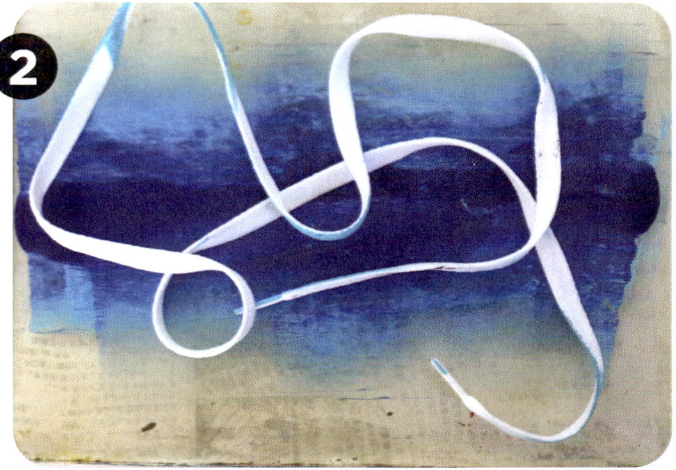

A second partial layer of paint and a repositioning of the shoe lace.

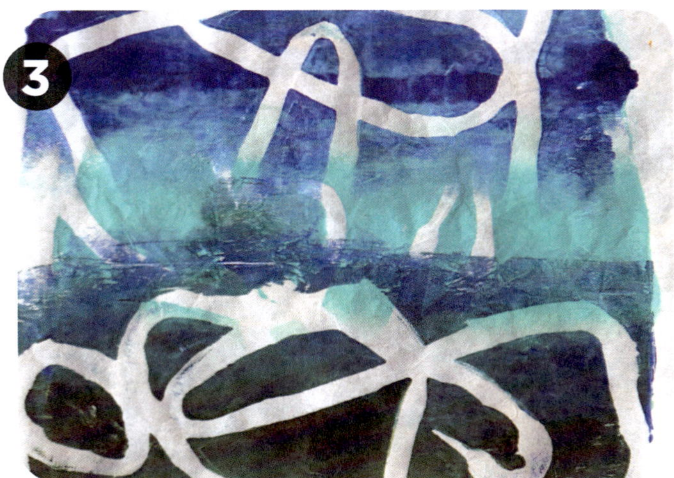

The layers are printed on white paper and not set to overlap, but rather to sit next to one another.

found objects

mark making and imprinting patterns

Marks can be made in the plate from any blunt object. I like to try writing with the eraser tip of a pencil, the end of my paint brush, a credit card corner, or my finger. All of the marks you make into the paint will transfer to the print when you press it into the paper, some more subtle than others. There are many interesting patterns in unusual places, like the bottom of your shoes, tile samples, jar lids, flip flops, and plastic containers. Think beyond the commercial art supply rubbing plate, the possibilities are endless!

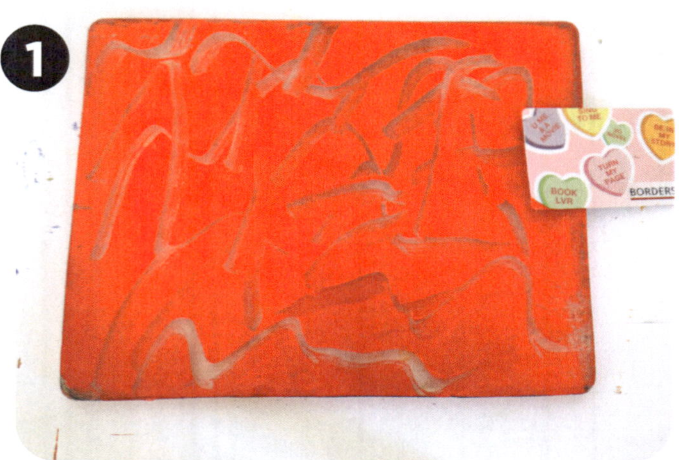

Using the corner of a gift card to make marks.

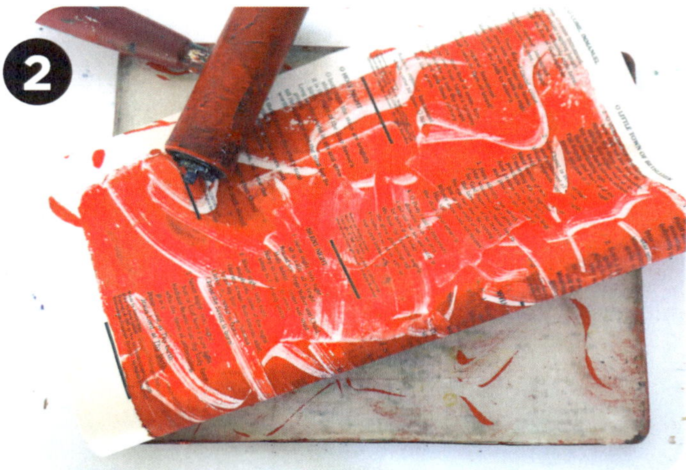

Pulling the print from the gift card pattern.

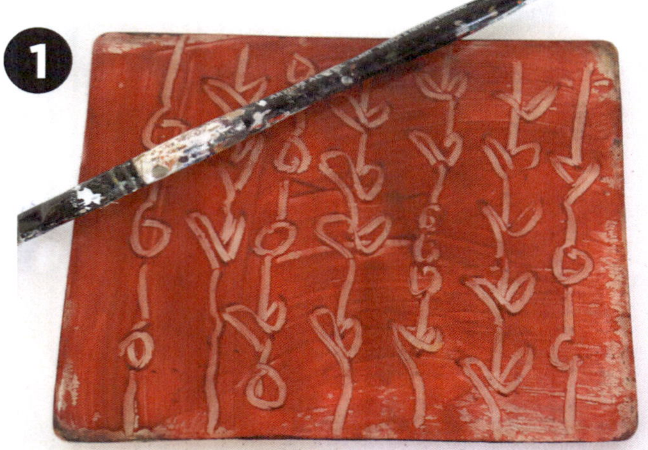

Drawing into the paint on the plate with the end of a paintbrush can yield spontaneous patterns.

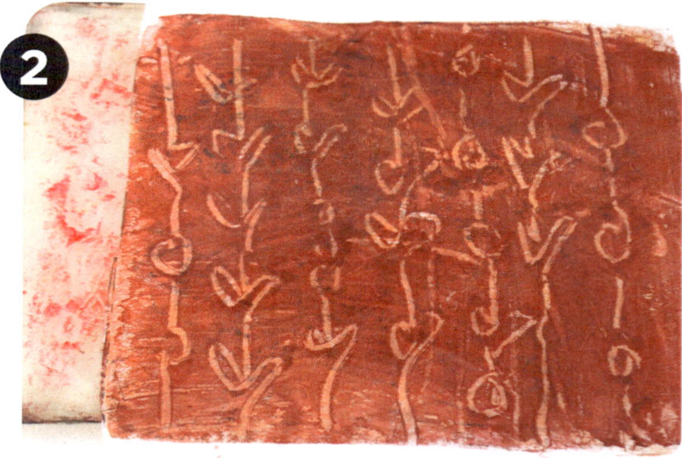

The print from the paintbrush marks. Note that the print is the mirror image of what is on the plate. Something to remember when writing letters.

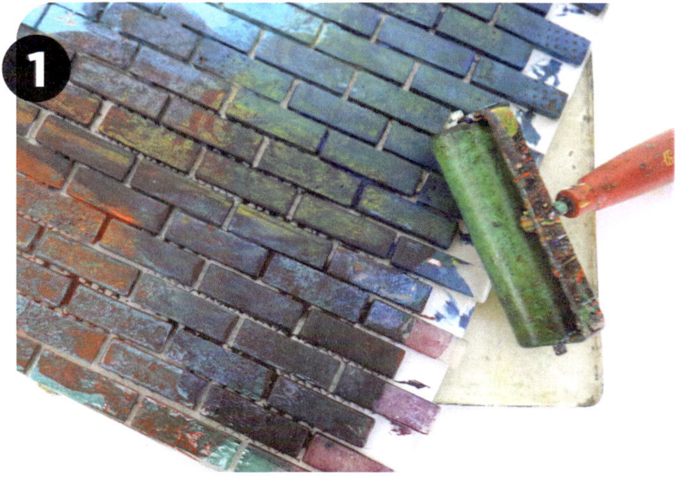

Tile samples from the hardware store in 12x12 sheets come in many different patterns.

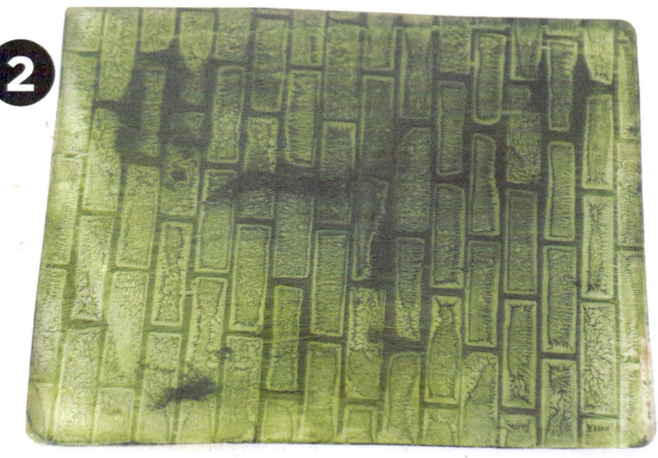

Tile can press into the paint on the plate to create subtle patterning.

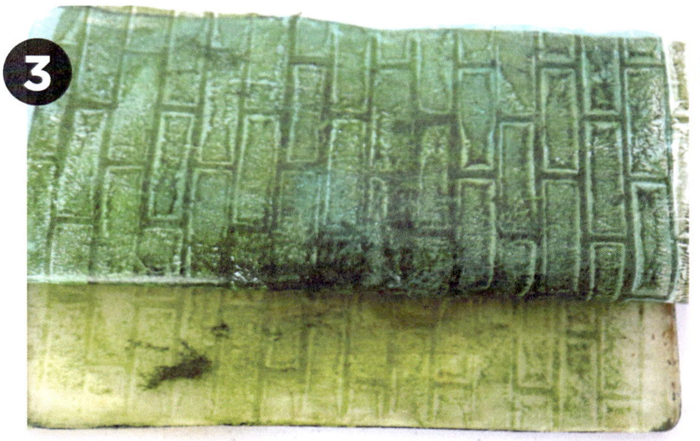

The print over a prepared light colored solid gives a two-tone subtle tile pattern.

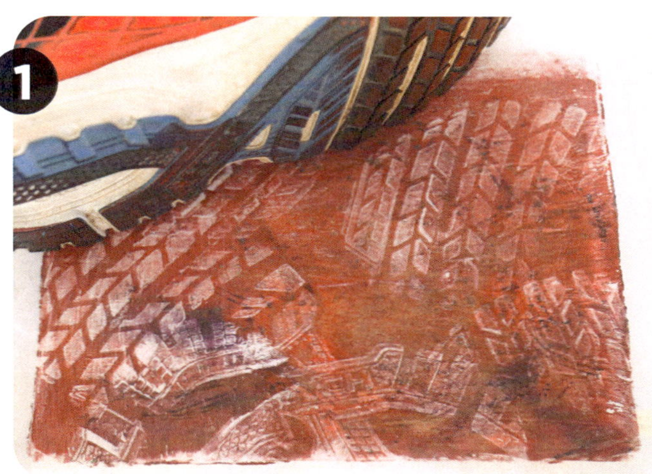

The pattern from the sole of my running shoe.

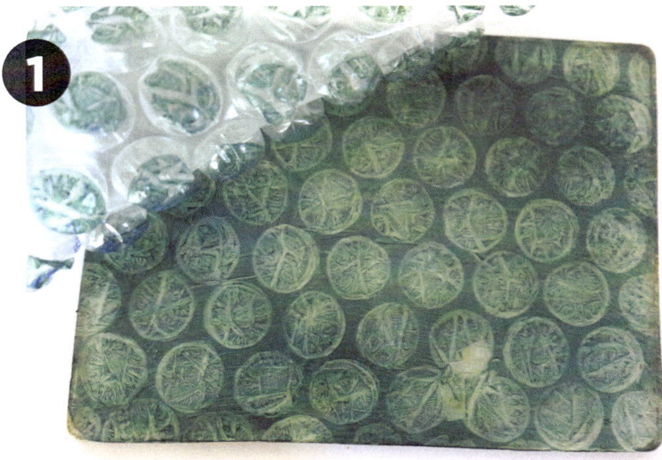

Bubble wrap from packaging comes in different sizes.

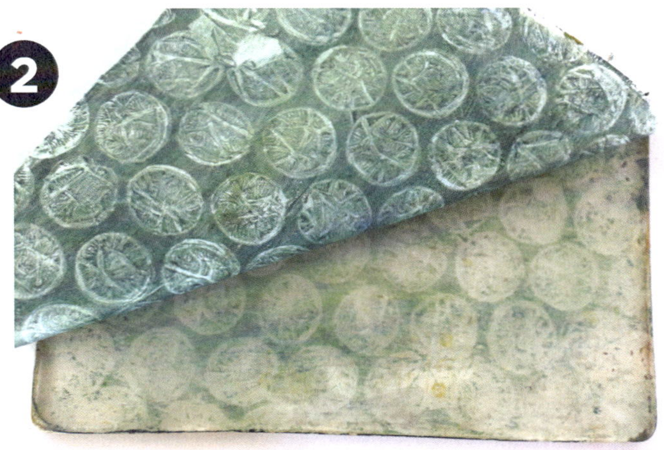

The print over a prepared light colored solid gives a two-tone subtle bubble pattern.

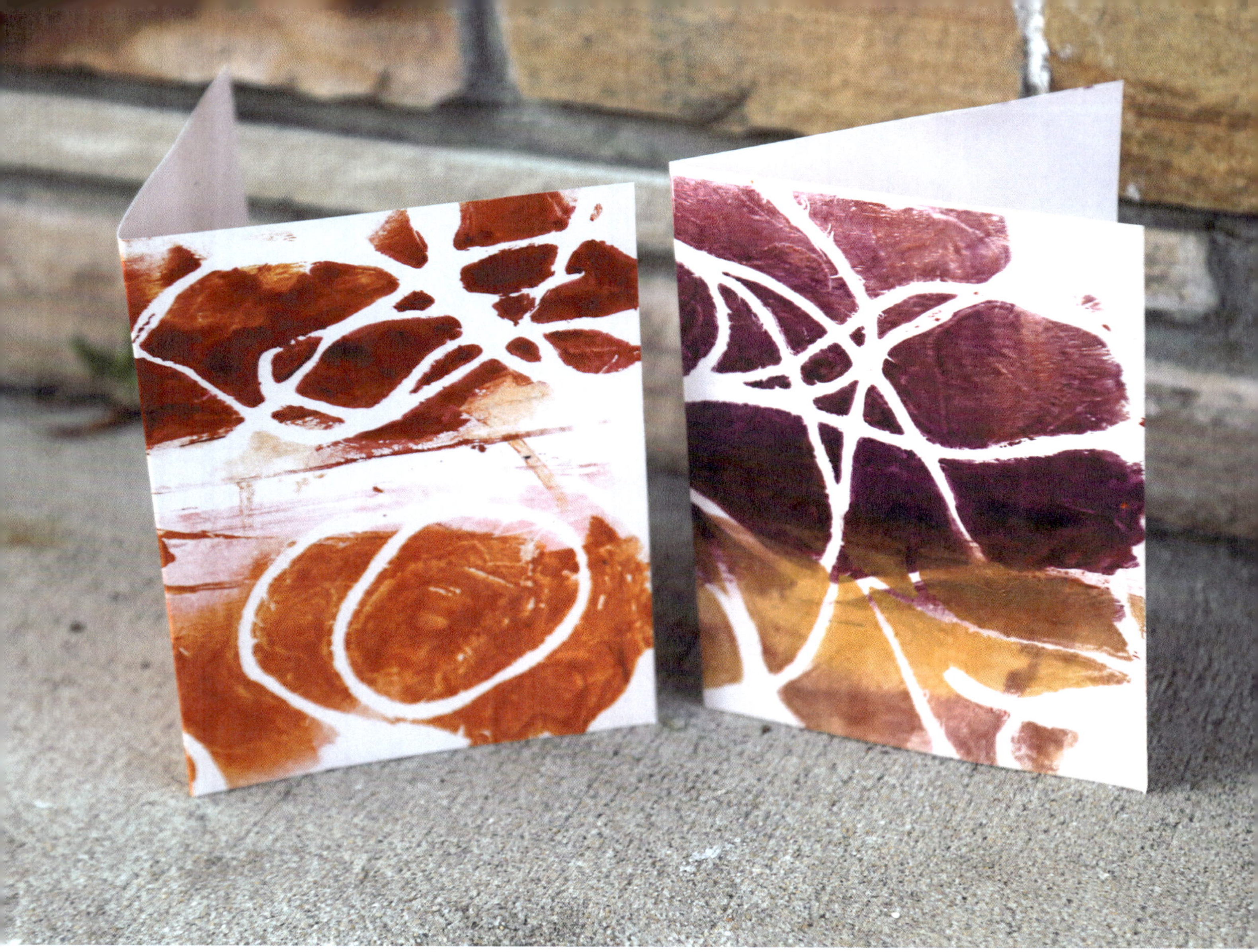

notes
cards and envelopes

What could be better than a hand-made card in these days of email and text exchange?

Use any of the techniques from this book to create your own original art note cards. The example above is simple string, but the possibilities are endless when you combine techniques.

I tend to get set up and print multiple sets of these cards—creating a stash that will carry me through several months. Write your own greetings for any occasion inside, your friends and family will thank you!

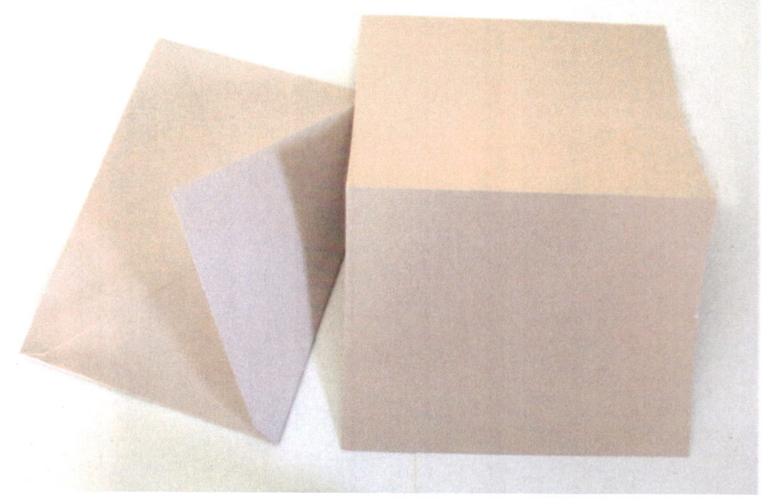

You can find blank note cards and matching envelopes in a wide variety of colors online or at your local Michael's store.

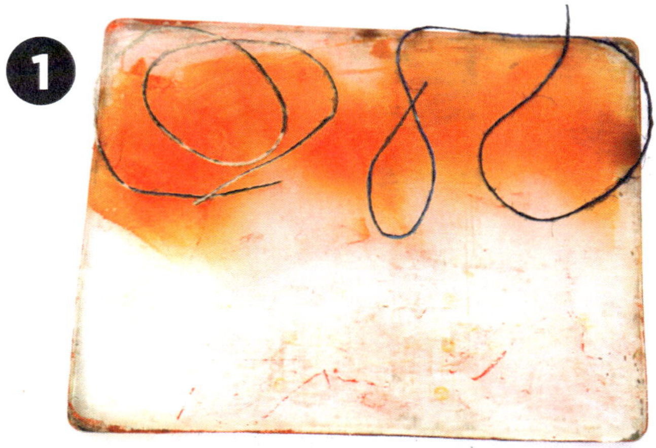

Laying the string into a stripe of
light golden brown paint.

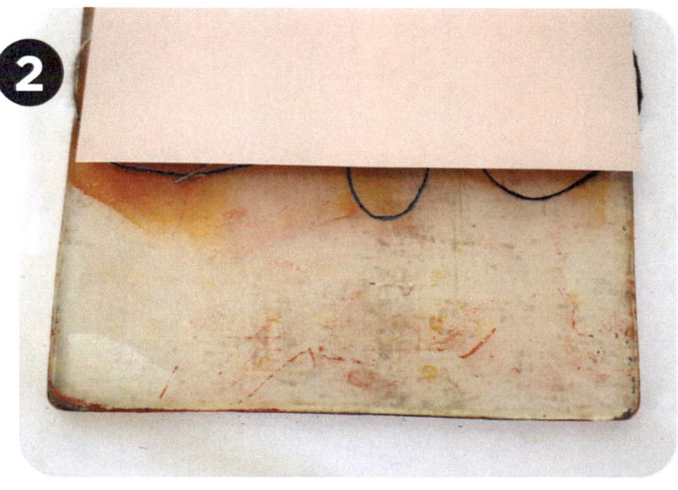

Laying the top edge of the card into the stripe of paint.

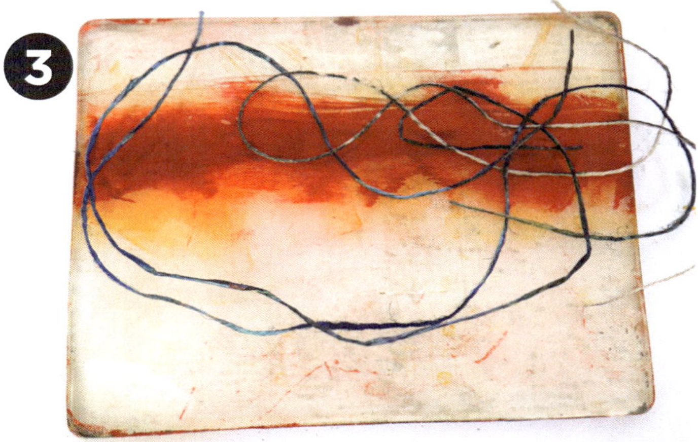

Adding a second dark stripe of paint with string.

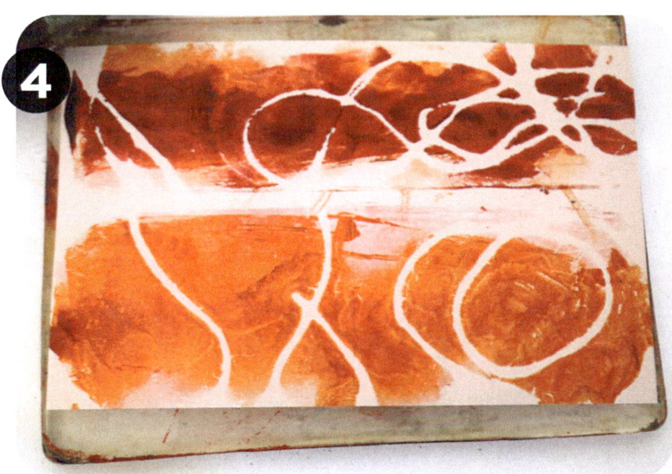

The double stripe with different strings.

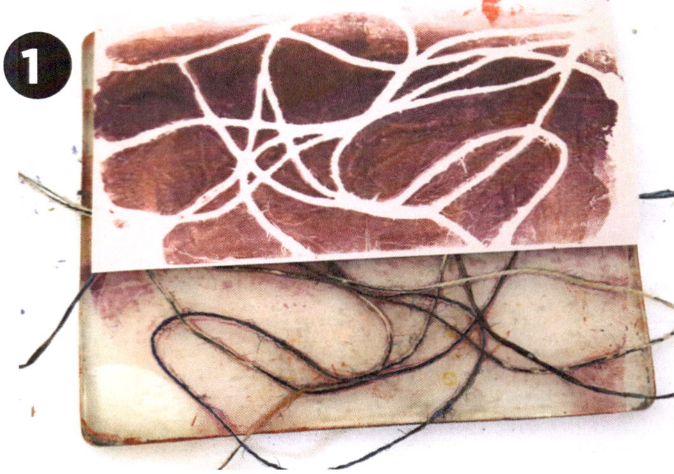

Layering dark purple paint with string over the
top edge of the pale pink blank note card stock.

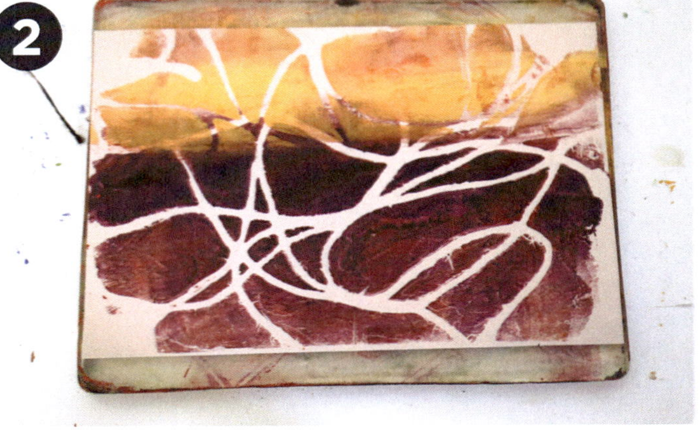

The double stripe with different string configurations,
dark purple and metallic gold stripes of paint.

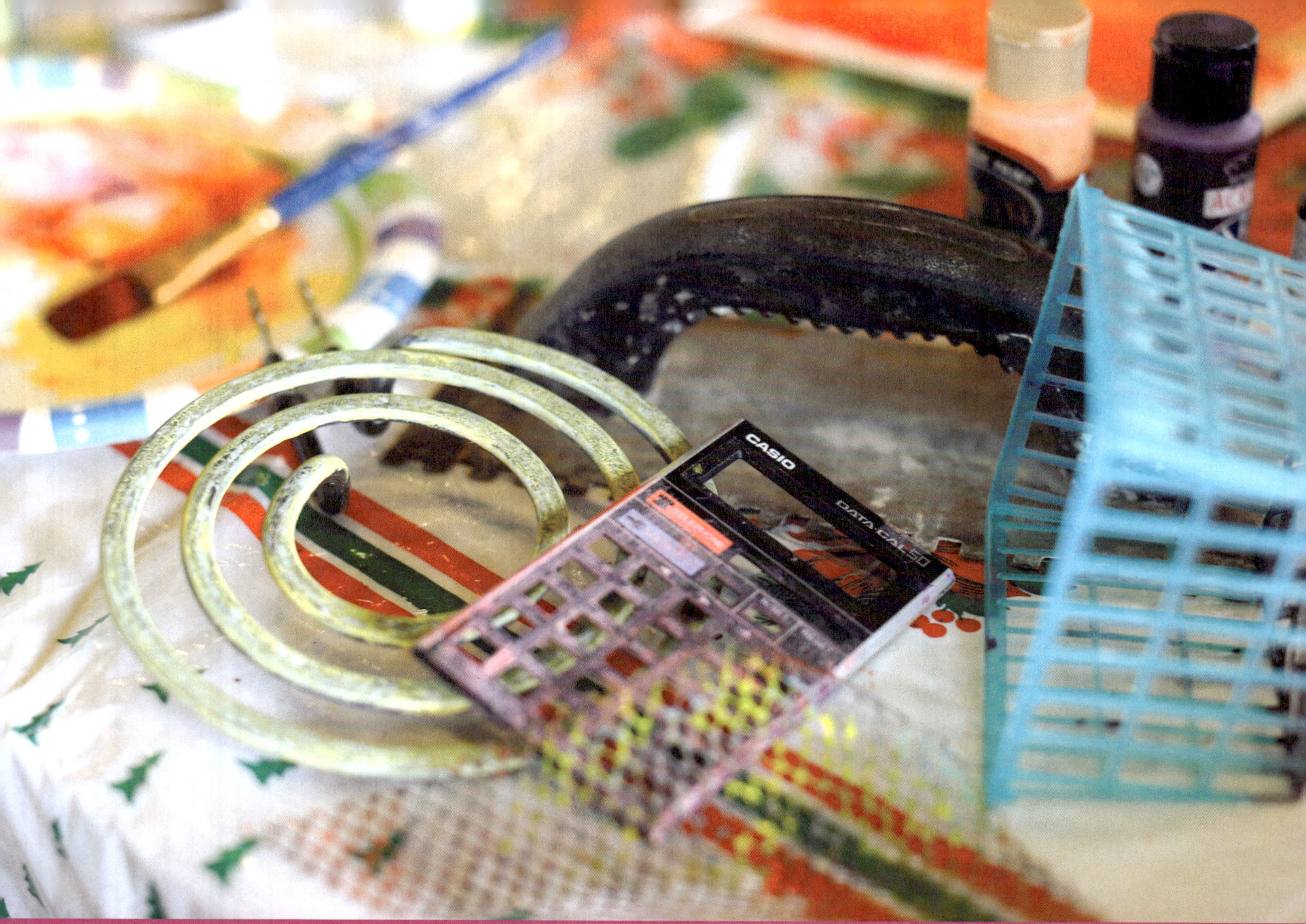

share the love

Old burner plates, calculator parts, berry baskets, tile trowels, flip-flop and sneaker soles, bubble wrap, yard sale finds... Some of my favorite techniques started out as happy accidents, some of my favorite stencils were not chosen by me, they were gifted to me. I learn from my students at the same time they are learning from me.

Experiment with combinations of the techniques presented in this book, mix and match to your heart's content. Don't be afraid to work on some crazy papers like gift tissue, old encyclopedias, altitude charts, street maps, and even your old grocery lists and bags.

When you come up with your absolute favorite technique, or have an *ah-ha moment*, let me know about it! Sharing is caring. Email me and tell me what you were inspired to create with your Gel Press printing plate.

elizabeth@PaperPaintings.com -- **I'd love to hear from you.**

When was the last time you did something for the first time?

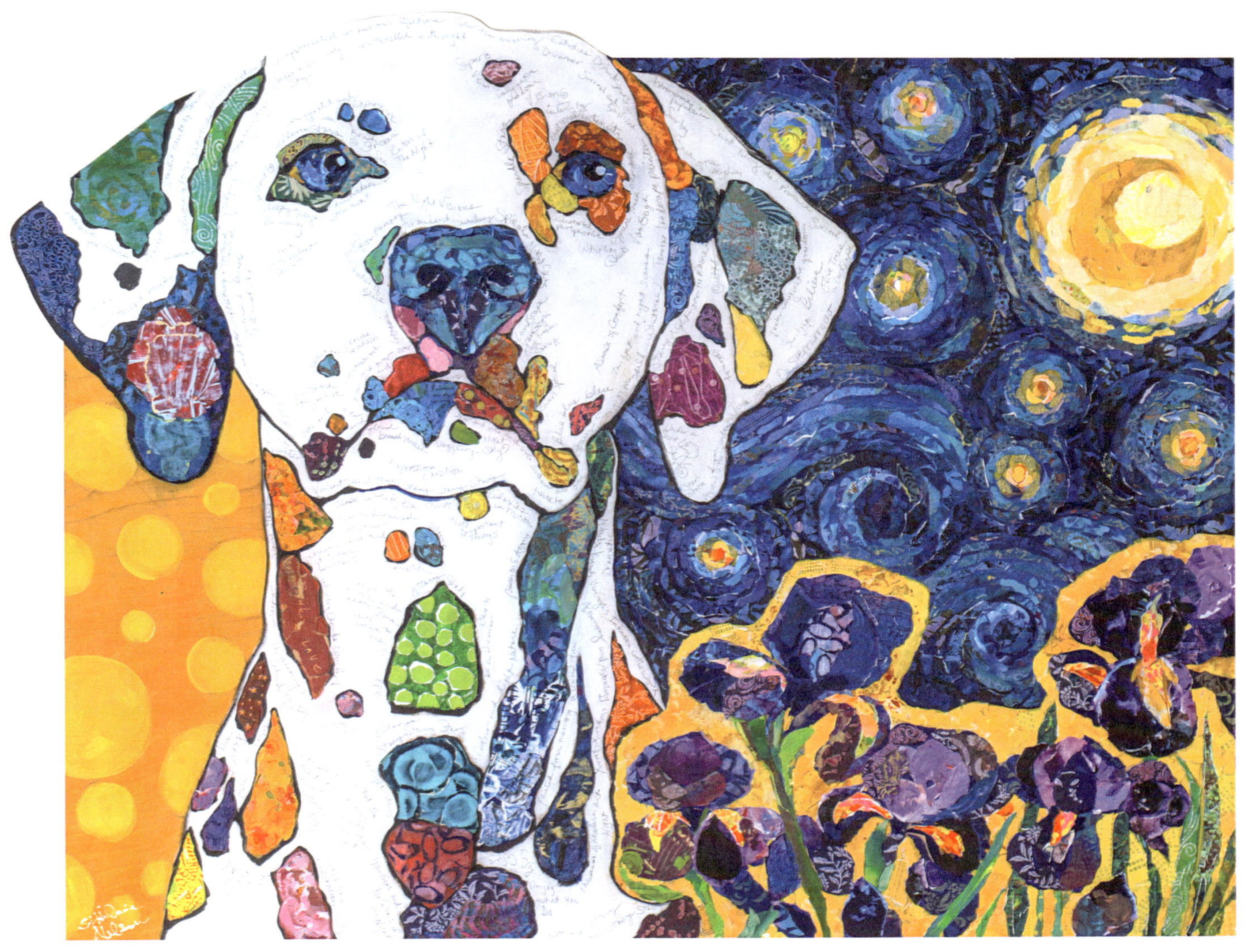

ABOUT THE AUTHOR

What sets the collage work of Elizabeth St. Hilaire apart is her use of unique, one-of-a-kind papers. Her signature collage style utilizes papers colored by hand, in every hue and texture needed to provide a complete paper palette.

View a full portfolio of the artists work at
PaperPaintings.com

Contact the artist via email at
Elizabeth@PaperPaintings.com

The Facebook studio page offers work in progress and workshop information
Facebook.com/PaperPaintingsCollageArtwork

Follow her Art Journey via the blog at
PaperPaintings.com

St. Hilaire is an Elite Blogger for *Growing Bolder*
PaperPaintings.GrowingBolder.com